PRAISE FOR *ATHEIST MIND, HUMANIST HEART*

"It is welcoming and refreshing to see a book on atheism that is not a polemic but a respectful and reasonable discussion of how a nonbeliever might engage the large questions that every human faces. Readers might discover that believers and humanist atheists share more in common than they think."

—Dudley Rose, associate dean at Harvard Divinity School

"*Atheist Mind, Humanist Heart* delivers compelling answers to the simple question of what we should each believe. This easily understandable yet profound guide will leave you inspired to define your own beliefs."

—Peter Boghossian, Portland State University,
author of *A Manual for Creating Atheists*

"The authors approach their very readable and engaging refurbishment of the Ten Commandments with wisdom, intelligence, accessibility, lucidity, and almost pious sensitivity. However, to increase the sum of human happiness, I would add one non-commandment to their ten: Thou shalt read this book!"

—Peter Atkins, Lincoln College, University of Oxford

"*Atheist Mind, Humanist Heart* exemplifies a welcome new trend in secular America—the turning of attention from all that's wrong with religion to a positive vision of what nonreligious people can be for and about. With clear heads and good hearts, Lex Bayer and John Figdor articulate a way to be secular that is not just rational but also compassionate and devoted to expanding the public good."

—Tom Krattenmaker, *USA Today* contributing columnist,
author of *The Evangelicals You Don't Know*

"What a smart and joyful read—like a flight over the terrain of my own mind and heart with intelligent guides to point out what I've never noticed before."

—Dale McGowan, 2008 Harvard Humanist of the Year, author
of *Parenting Beyond Belief, Raising Freethinkers,* and *Atheism for Dummies*

"Conversational, thoughtful, inviting. A very reasonable, very sound, and at times quite visionary offering."

—Phil Zuckerman, Pitzer College, author of *Living the Secular Life*

"An excellent book; worth reading regardless of one's religious or a-religious inclinations. Delicate, fair, courteous, the authors are expressing their humility and courage, not confrontation or condemnation. They face every issue in a penetrating, transparent, and down-to-earth way. It is unreservedly honest, written with genuineness, and holding nothing back."
—Raymond F. Paloutzian, coeditor of
Handbook of the Psychology of Religion and Spirituality, 2nd Edition

"*Atheist Mind, Humanist Heart* is a wonderful exploration of life as a religious skeptic. Truth, meaning, and fulfillment—Bayer and Figdor show that there is much awaiting those who step away from superstition and embrace life in the real world."
—David Niose, president of the Secular Coalition of America,
former president of the American Humanist Association,
author of *Nonbeliever Nation*

"I've devoted my adult life to encouraging everyone to check society's work: How do you know there is a god or gods? What makes you think that democracy is the best form of government? Figdor and Bayer have done a beautiful thing in *Atheist Mind, Humanist Heart* as they have presented their moral theory. They have shown their work. In doing so, they have presented moral problems as something that all people must and can engage personally. I love it!"
—August E. Brunsman IV, executive director of Secular Student Alliance

"With more and more young Americans abandoning organized religion today, toward what values and institutions can—and should—they turn to construct a morally coherent world? This gently voiced but finely crafted book offers answers that may surprise you and will certainly engage you. If you are among those who want to know more than what you *don't* believe, *Atheist Mind, Humanist Heart* offers a rich opportunity to discover what's worth believing—and why—in a world moving past traditional religious institutions and creeds."
—Richard Parker, Harvard Kennedy School

"Starting with a simple question, 'What do I believe?' the authors take us on a delightful journey to uncover the truth behind what forms our core beliefs."
—David Silverman, president of American Atheists

"This book is NOT the Ten Commandments 2.0. It's what you get when you use the tools of reason and humanism to rationally craft and promote better ways of life for everyone in the modern world and beyond."

—David Fitzgerald, author of *Nailed* and
The Complete Heretic's Guide to Western Religion

"Okay, so you've become an atheist. Now what? Read this book. That's my recommendation. It will help you build a new foundation for thinking and living a good life without God."

—John W. Loftus, author of *Why I Became an Atheist*
and *The Outsider Test for Faith*

"Atheists need to begin constructing positive principles to live by—and *Atheist Mind, Humanist Heart* provides a thorough demonstration of how to do just that."

—Paul Chiariello, cofounder of Yale Humanist Community,
editor of *Applied Sentience*

ATHEIST MIND, HUMANIST HEART

Rewriting the Ten Commandments for the Twenty-first Century

LEX BAYER AND JOHN FIGDOR

ROWMAN & LITTLEFIELD
Lanham • Boulder • New York • London

Published by Rowman & Littlefield
A wholly owned subsidary of The Rowman & Littlefield Publishing Group, Inc.
4501 Forbes Boulevard, Suite 200, Lanham, Maryland 20706
www.rowman.com

16 Carlisle Street, London W1D 3BT, United Kingdom

British Library Cataloguing in Publication Information Available

Library of Congress Cataloging-in-Publication Data

The hardback edition of this book was previously cataloged by the Library of Congress as follows:

Bayer, Lex.
  Atheist mind, humanist heart : rewriting the Ten commandments for the twenty-first century / Lex Bayer and John Figdor.
    pages cm
  Includes bibliographical references and index.
  ISBN 978-1-4422-3679-0 (cloth : alk. paper) — ISBN 978-1-4422-3680-6 (electronic) — ISBN 978-0-8108-9563-8 (paper : alk. paper)
    1. Atheism. 2. Conduct of life. 3. Ethics. I. Title.
  BL2747.3.B39 2014
  211'.8—dc23

                                                                2014025506

Printed in the United States of America

In tribute to:

My father, who taught me to have a curious mind
—*Lex Bayer*

My parents, for the education and
encouragement they gave me
—*John Figdor*

CONTENTS

INTRODUCTION:
QUESTIONING EVERYTHING

*In order to determine whether we can know anything with certainty,
we first have to doubt everything we know.*

—Descartes

LEX BAYER

I was standing in my high school synagogue in South Africa, waving my clenched fist in a circle above my head. Seven times we were supposed to wave a coin above our heads while chanting a special prayer.

I was fulfilling the Jewish practice of Kapparot. On the morning preceding Yom Kippur, the Day of Atonement, tens of thousands of Jews perform this ceremony. The ritual is supposed to transfer one's sins from oneself to the coin.

There I was, performing this ritual, surrounded by nearly nine hundred other students all twirling our hands above our heads and loudly chanting the same ancient prayer. Peering around at all those waving hands, my own twirls began to slow. *What am I doing?* I asked myself. *Why am I doing something so weird?*

I slowly lowered my hand. I just couldn't do it anymore.

The school was a secular Jewish day school. Science and literature were as much a part of the syllabus as Jewish studies. What had caused me and all these other well-educated, rational young adults to do something so strange, simply because we had been told to do so? As it turns out, the ritual is even more bizarre in its original (and still practiced) form—the believer swings not a coin but a live chicken.[1] Yes, the picture in your mind is correct—the more religious Jews swing a live chicken above their heads to

1

rid themselves of their sins. The coin is just a modern alternative for those without ready access to live poultry.

I can still picture myself standing in the synagogue, staring in disbelief at all those waving hands. That wasn't the first time in my life that I had questioned my religion. But on that day I crossed an invisible line, one that would change the way I acted and believed for the rest of my life. I decided from that moment forward that I would formulate my own beliefs and not just blindly adopt those of others.

Over the next several years, I tried to make sense of my religious doubts. What began with questioning Judaism soon expanded to questioning *all* religion and ultimately to questioning the very existence of God.

This last conclusion didn't come easily. I analyzed the arguments in favor of a belief in God, as well as the arguments against it, and wrestled with the ramifications of both for some time. In the end, I arrived at the only rational conclusion: God does not exist. I had become an atheist.

My acceptance that God does not exist didn't result in despair or anguish, as religious people often assume. Rather, like most new non-believers, I felt an initial wave of relief and liberation. Satisfaction, too. I had earnestly analyzed this mighty metaphysical question and arrived at a conclusion that I both understood and could rationalize. I felt the weight of thousands of years of religious belief lift from my shoulders. The comfort of knowledge remained.

Sadly, the comfort didn't last long. Soon I found myself facing an even bigger problem. I had figured out what I *didn't* believe, but I didn't know yet what I *could* believe. I discovered that while atheists are steadfast in denying the existence of a God, we often lack a strong assertion of the alternative—what exactly *do* atheists believe? Without a comprehensive system of assertive beliefs, I felt that any criticism of God and religion was spurious. The practicality of life requires that we each believe something. What is it that I believe?

When a colleague heard I had abandoned my belief in God, he challenged me to respond to the assertion, attributed to Christian apologist G. K. Chesterton, that "when a man stops believing in God, he doesn't then believe in nothing, he believes in anything."[2]

I'd like to say I fired back a witty response, but that wasn't the case. The claim brought me up short. I still had precious values, of course, but once the familiar religious foundations were stripped away, I didn't quite know how to ascribe any sanctity to those values. I was in effect living my life according to anything. Historian and author Will Durant, himself an atheist, offered a similar concern when he declared that "the greatest question of our time is not communism vs. individualism, not Europe vs.

America, not even the East vs. the West; it is whether man can bear to live without God."[3]

The more closely I looked at the values I'd acquired during the course of my life, the greater my awareness of the weakness of their foundation. I didn't know what I thought I knew. Without a belief in God—an almighty deity who decides what is right and what is wrong—how could I know why any value should be more or less valid than any other? How could I justify the continued importance of morality in my life? Should I even be moral?

JOHN FIGDOR

I was eight years old. It was snowing heavily in Scarsdale, New York, in the earliest hours of December 25, 1992. The light outside the window was casting a faint yellow glow on the frosted glass, but I wasn't focused on the still beauty of this Christmas night. Instead, crouched at the top of the stairs like a cat burglar, I peeked through the banister toward the living room. Muted conversation filtered up the stairs, along with some rustling in our downstairs hall closet, just out of view.

I crept down one step, two steps, three steps, like a ninja in footie pajamas, until at last the hall closet came into view. I saw my mom and dad chatting quietly as they retrieved the Christmas presents from their secret hiding spot in the closet and placed them under the tree in our living room. I crouched in the shadows, my heart beating out of my chest. I'd just caught my parents in flagrante delicto putting presents under the tree! I gloated silently. I had definitive proof I could share with my friends. As I watched, my dad took a bite out of one of the cookies I'd left for Santa before returning to the hall closet to collect a few more presents.

I wouldn't say that disbelieving in Santa made me an atheist, but it did make me realize three things: first, things aren't always what they seem or what people say they are; second, supernatural explanations are suspect; and finally, if you want to find out the truth, you can't just go asking other people—you have to investigate for yourself.

That Christmas night episode was the first of a long series of insights that slowly transitioned me from a believing Christian to an atheist. What began with belief in a naïve version of Christianity (often referred to in divinity schools as "Sunday school Christianity") was irrevocably damaged that night with the discovery that Santa wasn't real.

My faith in Christianity continued to diminish during high school, especially during confirmation class in the United Church of Christ, the church in which I was raised. Confirmation class was required for all fourteen-year-olds who wanted to become members. The class was led by a wonderfully progressive Christian minister who didn't shrink from addressing the controversial parts of the Bible. We would have Bible readings and discuss them, talking about what we found compelling and what we found suspicious.

As the class progressed, I realized that I found most of the book tedious and the rest of it morally and factually suspect.

It was in this class that I abandoned my faith altogether. The occasion was a discussion on the problem of evil—or why bad things happen to good people. As it happens, I was studying the Holocaust at the same time in my social studies class at school. During the discussion, my faintly Christian beliefs were utterly unable to explain why a benevolent God would allow the radical evil of the Holocaust to happen. Worse, I discovered apologists arguing all sorts of insane things, such as:

- Jews deserved the Holocaust for being insufficiently holy.[4]
- The Bible's answer was in the Book of Job, which suggests that human beings cannot question God's morality because God's infinite ways are so far beyond our human comprehension.[5]

I was appalled. The absence of intellectual rigor in the arguments, the transparent lack of real compassion for the victims of the Holocaust, and the inability of the apologists even to consider the possibility of God's culpability in the world's horrors[6] opened my eyes to the lack of serious answers to this critical problem. The deeper I dug, the worse it became. Not only did I discover a foundational problem with Christian theology (the assertion that God is omnibenevolent, or "perfectly good") but, worse, I found myself turned off by a church that seemed more interested in preserving the dignity and moral purity of God than concerned for the systematic murder of millions.

But in turning away from one problem, I found myself facing another. I had discarded my religious faith but found myself asking the question, "Now what?" After all, realizing that there isn't an omniscient, omnipotent, omnibenevolent deity watching over the good and punishing the wicked is just the first step. Having figured out what I didn't believe in, I now had to investigate what I *should* believe in. I found myself faced with a whole new set of questions:

- How does morality work without God?
- If I'm not a pawn in God's experiment, what should I do with my life?

- How can I tell what is true and what is false?
- What happens after you die?

I dived into these questions as a philosophy major at Vassar College, then volunteered in a domestic violence shelter in Butte, Montana. But the big questions continued to rattle around in my mind, and after a year in Montana I enrolled in Harvard Divinity School. Before long, I was serving as president of the Harvard Atheists, Skeptics, and Humanists society.

I began to notice that students were less interested in debating the question of whether God exists than in discussing what to do and how to live. I recall a conversation with Harvard's humanist chaplain, Greg Epstein, in which we agreed that while the question, "Does God exist?" was pretty well covered in books, articles, and blogs, the question, "What should one then believe?" was more important and more interesting for young nonbelievers. Helping to answer that question, I decided, was the best way I could help my fellow nonbelievers.

In 2010, I was appointed the humanist chaplain serving Stanford University. Being a humanist chaplain, I interact with lots of students and so am confronted with the most significant questions and concerns facing young nonbelievers. Just as at Harvard, at Stanford the negatives are already well established. These students reject blind faith, whether in God, prophets, or the government. They reject creationism and its rebranded doppelgänger, "intelligent design." But despite all that, there is still a real need in the young atheist community to answer the question of what nonbelievers *do* believe in.

★ ★ ★

And so, in pursuing very different lives, we, the two authors of this book, having abandoned our faiths, found ourselves confronted with the same question: *What do we believe now?*

Partial answers to this question abound—a book chapter here, a blog post there. But we've yet to find a book that comprehensively answers this simple question in an intuitive and nontechnical way. It is a challenge for all nonbelievers, but it is an especially unfortunate gap for college students during the years when many first begin to seriously ask the big questions and to challenge their faith.

It was in part to help answer this question that coauthor John Figdor became a humanist (or atheist) chaplain. To some, especially believers, the very idea of a humanist chaplain is a contradiction in terms—after all, why would students who do not believe in God want or need a chaplain?

John posed this very question to Greg Epstein, the humanist chaplain at Harvard, while he was a student there. As is his habit, Epstein answered the question with a series of questions:

> Don't students who are nonreligious deserve to have a nonjudgmental person to talk to about problems such as adjusting to life away from one's parents, coping with the intense academic environment, and coming to terms with sickness or death in the family? Don't nonreligious students deserve to have a person on campus organizing interesting education programs and charity drives? Don't nonreligious students deserve a representative to ensure that their perspectives are welcomed on campus?

When John found himself answering "yes" to all of these questions, he knew that he was on a path to becoming a humanist chaplain himself. But even then he knew the title "humanist chaplain" wasn't ideal. After all, "chaplain" is generally understood to be a fundamentally religious word, meaning a priest or minister. The term doesn't really describe him. He is neither a priest nor a minister but a community organizer, friend, and advocate for nonreligious students. But the term chaplain is so ubiquitous in our educational system that nonreligious advocates such as John are forced for practical reasons to accept the title, however awkward it may be. If a special term were invented like "councilor" or "advisor," that name would be given second-class status. Chaplaincies tend to have a special status and administrative privileges within most university structures, so adopting the chaplain nomenclature creates an equal and alternative voice to that of traditional religions on campus.

As an interesting aside, the history of the term "chaplain" has been one of expanding definitions. In the beginning, only Christian chaplains were allowed on the Harvard campus. But as time passed, Jews were eventually welcomed into the fraternity of college and university chaplains, followed much later by Hindu, Muslim, Buddhist, Jain, and Sikh chaplains. Now colleges such as Harvard and Stanford have more than thirty chaplains, representing a vast diversity of religious and *nonreligious* beliefs.[7]

As the biographies that opened this book underscore, we grew up on different continents with very different upbringings. John trained as an analytic philosopher, religious studies scholar, and college chaplain, while Lex was educated in engineering and technology entrepreneurship. When we met at Stanford, we quickly found that, despite our different backgrounds and perspectives, our ways of thinking were surprisingly similar.

We both have an interest in philosophy, debate, rigorous logic, and skepticism—classic characteristics of the atheist mind. We also both care deeply about compassionate ethics, personal integrity, society, and morals—our humanist hearts. Between the two, as our own stories show, lies a gap that still remains to be filled, not just for our own lives but also for the atheist and humanist community.

This book is the result of our combined efforts to fill the void of disbelief that remains after a rejection of God by answering the questions, "What should one believe after abandoning faith?" and "What are the positive principles of atheism?" We have decided to answer these challenges in an unorthodox way—by updating the Ten Commandments to a version for the twenty-first century, a version that reflects modern secular thought, science, psychology, and philosophy. A version that is intellectually rigorous but easily understandable, reflecting both the atheist mind and the humanist heart. Our goal is to provide a clear and comprehensive framework of secular beliefs about life, human behavior, and ethics. We call our version Ten Non-commandments for the Twenty-first Century.

Why "non-commandments"? Because a defining difference between our version and the original is that ours are amendable. Our non-commandments are not written in stone, nor do we pretend that these are the only valid answers to the challenge of meaning without God. Rather, they are our best attempt to answer these questions as we see them today, at this point in our own atheist and humanist lives, and to be as transparent as possible in our explanations of our arguments.

In writing this book, we encountered something that will be familiar to many readers: the difference between an idea in thought and an idea in words. Just as we often realize something makes no sense only after we say it aloud, thoughts that seemed lucid and strong in our minds often showed their flaws once they were committed to the page. The exercise of writing down our beliefs helped us truly discover our beliefs and how they all tie together.

We enthusiastically invite the reader to join us in this conversation. This is not a sermon from two guys with all the answers, but a dialogue by two questioning, flawed individuals about the most important questions we face as human beings. We hope that our thoughts may serve as a useful reference for the many nonbelievers out there. But even more important, we hope to encourage you and others to reflect on your own beliefs. We hope that you will add to our work and discover your own personal non-commandments, and that together we might all attain a deeper understanding of our innermost beliefs.

1

REWRITING THE
TEN COMMANDMENTS

*Say what you will about the Ten Commandments, you must always
come back to the pleasant fact that there are only ten of them.*

—H. L. Mencken

An atheist, an agnostic, and a humanist walk into a restaurant . . .

We'll begin with some definitions. What is the difference between
atheists, agnostics, and humanists? First off, we should acknowledge
that these terms have precise philosophical definitions as well as popular
meanings in society. Since this book is aimed at a nontechnical audience,
we'll be referring to the popular uses of these terms.

ATHEIST, AGNOSTIC, HUMANIST

Atheists do not believe in a God or gods. Agnostics say they don't know
whether a God or gods exist, and many go further to say that the existence
of a deity or deities is unknowable. On first glance, it may seem as if these
are two distinct categories, but it is actually possible for one person to be
both an atheist and an agnostic. In fact, it's extremely common.

Atheists do not believe in a God, but that doesn't mean they claim to
be certain. Though years of thought and study often lead atheists to be extremely confident in their conclusions, it's very rare to find one who claims
to have definitive proof that God does not exist. If someone asked you
your age, you would answer with full confidence. But if someone asked if
there were any possibility that you were wrong, no matter how slight—any

chance you have been mistaken all these years, that your birth certificate had an error, or that a massive conspiracy in your family hid the fact that you are actually one year older than you thought—you would probably have to admit that, yes, there was a tiny chance that you were wrong, a chance that's so small that it wasn't worth mentioning.

That is how most atheists feel about God.

Most agnostics have views that are impossible to distinguish from most atheists, but they choose to emphasize the doubt, while the atheists choose to emphasize their confidence. That is why it is possible and common for an atheist to also be an agnostic and an agnostic to also be an atheist. Each has simply chosen to emphasize a different aspect of his or her belief.

The commonality between the beliefs of atheists and agnostics is much greater than the differences. Both groups recognize that extraordinary claims require extraordinary evidence,[1] and both agree that there isn't extraordinary evidence for the existence of God. The difference is that the atheist moves from the recognition that extraordinary evidence for the existence of God hasn't been presented to the confident (but not certain) belief that God probably doesn't exist.

For his book *The God Delusion*, prominent atheist biologist Richard Dawkins created a useful seven-point scale to express the degrees of religious belief and doubt. Scoring a one on the scale indicates a person's absolute certainty that God exists. A seven indicates absolute certainty that God does *not* exist. In both these two instances (a one and a seven on the scale), the person is saying that no new information could ever change his or her mind. (Think back to the example of knowing your age to see how foolish that would be.)

Someone who identifies on the scale as a two believes God exists but stops short of claiming absolute certainty. A three is a little less certain; four is exactly in the middle; a five leans toward doubt; and a six indicates a strong confidence (but not certainty) that God does not exist.

Even Dawkins himself, who is probably the most well-known atheist alive today, calls himself a six on the scale, not a seven (a 6.9, to be more specific[2]). When an interviewer a few years ago asked him why he doesn't call himself an agnostic, he said, "Well, I *am* an agnostic." The papers the next day broke the story: "The world's most famous atheist admits that he is actually an agnostic!" But saying that Dawkins "admits" to being an agnostic is like saying a Christian "admits" to being a Baptist or a Methodist. "Baptist" or "Methodist" simply emphasizes different aspects that a person who believes in Jesus decides to identify with. The same is usually true for an atheist and agnostic.

The media made a story out of Dawkins's statement because most people (mainly religious believers) think agnostic means a four on the scale—someone who thinks there is an equal chance (fifty-fifty) that God exists or does not exist. But as we've already noted, people who self-identify as agnostics are usually deeply skeptical of the possibility of God's existence. If pressed, they typically would say that they think that God is a low- or very-low-probability hypothesis, putting them at a five or a six on the scale.

But because they are assumed to be smack in the middle, agnostics are often accused of being wishy-washy and fence-sitters. And because atheists are assumed to be sevens, they are often accused of being closed-minded or arrogant. One of the goals of this book is to change these misconceptions and remove the stigma from self-identifying as an atheist or agnostic.

Why do we call ourselves atheists? Because we agree with Dawkins when he further argues that people who declare that they are agnostic about the existence of God should be similarly agnostic about the existence of fairies at the bottom of the garden. If an agnostic claims that we have to hold out making a judgment about whether God exists, then we should be equally careful to declare our doubts about knowing whether or not fairies exist. But most of us are very comfortable saying outright that we do not believe in these fantasies, emphasizing our confidence rather than the sliver of doubt. We feel little need to clarify that, while the probability of fairies existing is extremely low, in principle it is not possible to completely disprove their existence. For this reason, Dawkins also describes himself as a de facto atheist.[3]

You may wonder, as we have, why so many people grant God a benefit of doubt that is not extended to analogous beings such as fairies (or Santa or Bigfoot). On reflection, we see three main reasons. First, God is typically portrayed as having measures at his disposal to punish doubters and nonbelievers. The fear of punishment—including going to hell for eternity, or at least exclusion from the possibility of going to heaven—can lead many of us to want to hedge our bets just a little. Second, the possibility that a higher, all-knowing power is somehow guiding our lives for the best might feel comforting. Third, religion plays an enormous role in society. In the United States its role is reinforced through the Pledge of Allegiance and the printing of "In God We Trust" on our currency. Since the majority of people in the world are religious believers, there is often public pressure to conform, and questioning the existence of God is socially discouraged in many places.

Where do humanists fit into this picture? Humanists are people who think that they can lead a life of meaning and value without a belief in

God or the supernatural. Humanists stress the goodness of human beings, emphasize common human needs, and seek rational ways of solving human problems. Essentially, humanists are atheists and agnostics who, in addition to having serious doubts about the existence of God, also emphasize and promote values such as empathy, compassion, social justice, critical thinking, and science literacy.

While we have discussed these labels to help clarify the terms we are using, the similarities among these three perspectives are far greater than their differences. As it turns out, most atheists and agnostics are humanists, most humanists are atheist and agnostic, and most agnostics do not believe in God.

Now we can finish the joke at the beginning of the chapter: An atheist, an agnostic, and a humanist walk into a restaurant . . . and the hostess says, "Table for one?"

STATEMENTS OF SECULAR BELIEF

The Ten Commandments are the foundation of Judeo-Christian beliefs. The Bible teaches that these Ten Commandments were delivered directly by God to Moses on Mount Sinai.[4] God engraved these laws onto two stone tablets that Moses then delivered to the people of Israel. These commandments are said to be the word of God and are among the core pillars of faith for believers.

The atheist worldview lacks a similar set of statements expressing the most important secular beliefs—statements of what atheists do believe. That is what we intend to do in the pages ahead.

Many atheist groups, personalities, and bloggers have created statements of belief in the past. A few of the more notable examples include the Humanist Manifesto I, II, and III created by the American Humanist Association (AHA)[5] and the Minimum Statement by the International Humanist and Ethical Union (IHEU).[6] On the humorous side are the Penn Commandments[7] by magician Penn Jillette, George Carlin's reduction of the original Ten Commandments to two,[8] and Christopher Hitchens's version, whose eighth commandment is a passionate plea to turn off your cell phone.[9]

However, our list differs from these in a few important ways. We begin by spelling out our assumptions, then justify each belief with a rationale for each claim. Along the way, we work from two guiding principles woven tightly into the atheist mind-set: that all claims must be supported by evidence and that all arguments should be logically consistent.

This isn't how such lists are usually built, of course. Most beliefs are sourced to an authority—whether the Bible, a revered teacher, the Pope, or Mom and Dad—and believed because that authority is held in high regard. Ours is a different approach, a list based not on a top-down authority but built from the bottom up on evidence and justification. This is similar to constructing a high-rise building. First a solid foundation is laid. Only when that foundation is deemed solid and level is the first floor added to it. Each floor is inspected carefully in turn before the next is added, and the next, until the building is complete.

So too will the atheist framework of belief start by constructing a fundamental foundation and then layering additional "floors" of beliefs upon it. Each layer of belief will be explored and justified before adding additional layers. The higher floors will offer panoramic views into the world of ethics and morality. Because all of our beliefs and assumptions are articulated in our reasoning process, we are confident that each new floor is placed on a solid understructure. And because our reasons will be articulated out loud, you won't have to take our word for it—you can decide for yourself if any false assumptions are present.

The biblical Ten Commandments are said to be the work of God. As such, they are held to be indisputable and sacred, requiring no justification. By comparison, the Ten Non-commandments we outline claim no sanctity or authority. They are the nonholy, nonabsolutist work of two self-reflecting atheists. They are meant to be debated, examined, and improved on. As two individuals in a community of millions, we claim no special authority, position, or jurisdiction to write down such a list. We can't even declare that they speak for the atheist community at large. Rather, our intent is to demonstrate the process that two highly motivated atheists pursued in order to arrive at our best effort for the list of Ten Non-commandments for the Twenty-first Century. In formulating these beliefs, we have attempted to be deliberately transparent, rational, and honest in our approach so as to lay bare our inner thoughts, logic, and biases.

We decided to take the time and energy to understand what our core beliefs are and where they come from. Not being able to clearly express our most important beliefs felt like an abdication of our responsibility to engage the world honestly. While our initial intent was to decide for ourselves which beliefs we should hold and the reasons for those beliefs, we also have another motivation: we hope to encourage and convince you to formulate and reflect on your *own* beliefs. After we walk you through our process, chapter 12 will guide you through the process of committing your own beliefs to paper. We hope this book will be the catalyst for you to seek out a deep understanding of your personal beliefs and for you to find your own Ten Non-commandments. If the unexamined life is not worth living, then the unexamined belief is not worth holding or acting on.

A BRIEF LOOK AT THE ORIGINALS

The Judeo-Christian Ten Commandments are described in the Bible in Exodus (20:1–17) and again in Deuteronomy (5:1–21). Many people are surprised (as you may be soon) when they read the actual passages. For such an important statement of beliefs, they're a bit of a mess—nothing like the Ten Commandments most of us learned when we were young. The lists you've seen carved into stone monuments are loose abbreviations of the originals. The biblical commandments aren't neatly demarcated into ten sections, and the passages themselves contain more than ten imperative statements. The original verses are also less restrained than the Sunday school version: they include colorful language about the consequences for those who do not follow them.

Religious groups differ slightly in how they arrange the commandments, as well as how they rephrase them, although the differences are subtle. The full version of the biblical commandments as listed and grouped in Exodus (20:1–17) in the King James Bible[10] is as follows:

I.   *I am the Lord thy God, which have brought thee out of the land of Egypt, out of the house of bondage. Thou shalt have no other gods before me.*

II.   *Thou shalt not make unto thee any graven image, or any likeness of any thing that is in heaven above, or that is in the earth beneath, or that is in the water under the earth. Thou shalt not bow down thyself to them, nor serve them: for I the Lord thy God am a jealous God, visiting the iniquity of the fathers upon the children unto the third and fourth generation of them that hate me; And shewing mercy unto thousands of them that love me, and keep my commandments.*

III.   *Thou shalt not take the name of the Lord thy God in vain; for the Lord will not hold him guiltless that taketh his name in vain.*

IV.   *Remember the sabbath day, to keep it holy. Six days shalt thou labour, and do all thy work: But the seventh day is the sabbath of the Lord thy God: in it thou shalt not do any work, thou, nor thy son, nor thy daughter, thy manservant, nor thy maidservant, nor thy cattle, nor thy stranger that is within thy gates: For in six days the Lord made heaven and earth, the sea, and all that in them is, and rested the seventh day: wherefore the Lord blessed the sabbath day, and hallowed it.*

V.   *Honor thy father and thy mother: that thy days may be long upon the land which the Lord thy God giveth thee.*

VI.   *Thou shalt not kill.*

VII.   *Thou shalt not commit adultery.*

VIII.   *Thou shalt not steal.*

IX.   *Thou shalt not bear false witness against thy neighbour.*

X.   *Thou shalt not covet thy neighbour's house, thou shalt not covet thy neighbour's wife, nor his manservant, nor his maidservant, nor his ox, nor his ass, nor any thing that is thy neighbour's.*

A bit different than you remember them? Take the second commandment. It's usually abbreviated as, "Thou shalt not make unto thee any graven image." But, it actually goes on to enumerate much broader prohibitions, and further adds a less-than-veiled threat of God's punishment for its violation.

The commandments can be divided into two sections. The first four deal mostly with the relationship between God and humans, while the rest deal with the ethics of human relationships. Our Ten Non-commandments for the Twenty-first Century will also be divided into two sections. The first set will deal with beliefs about the world—what exists, what's true, and what's false. These beliefs will satisfy the atheist mind, which values reason, observational data, and evidence. The second set will focus on ethics—how we should behave and treat each other. These beliefs will satisfy the humanist heart, which values human interactions, community, and society.

Now it's time to start constructing Ten Non-commandments for the Twenty-first Century.

I

A FRAMEWORK FOR FACTS

2

THE PARADOX OF BELIEF

"Begin at the beginning," the King said, very gravely, "and go on till you come to the end: then stop."

—Lewis Carroll, *Alice in Wonderland*

We begin by suggesting a framework of secular belief. It begins with the simple question, *How can I justify any of my beliefs?*

When thinking about why we believe in anything, we quickly realize that every belief is based on other preexisting beliefs. Consider, for example, the belief that brushing our teeth keeps them healthy. Why do we believe this? Because brushing helps removes plaque buildup that causes teeth to decay.

But why do we believe plaque causes decay? Because our dentists, teachers, and parents told us so. Why do we trust what our dentist says? Because other dentists and articles and books we've read confirmed it. Why do we believe those accounts? Because they presented many more pieces of information confirming the link between plaque, bacterial growth, and tooth decay. And why do we believe *those* pieces of information?

There seems to be no end. It's like the old story of a learned man giving a public lecture in which he mentions that the earth orbits the sun.[1] At the end of the lecture an elderly lady approaches the lectern and sternly informs him that he is wrong: the world, she says, is actually resting on the back of a giant turtle. The learned man smiles and asks, "What is the turtle standing on?" The old lady doesn't even blink and replies, "Another turtle, of course!" When the learned man starts to respond, "And what is *that* turtle—" she interrupts him: "You're very clever, young man . . . but it's turtles all the way down!"

19

Just like that cosmic stack of turtles, the process of justifying beliefs based on other beliefs never ends—unless at some point we manage to arrive at a belief that doesn't rely on justification from any prior belief. That would be a foundational source of belief.

But this creates a paradox of its own: we can only justify a belief by basing it ultimately on source beliefs, and source beliefs by definition have no justifying beliefs. So the only way to justify a particular belief is to start with an unjustifiable belief.

It's like getting down to the last turtle to find it resting on . . . nothing at all.

How maddening! Instead of clarifying how we can decide what to believe, we've instead proven that the only way to justify beliefs is to acknowledge that certain principles must be accepted without justification.

But if we can't justify these source beliefs, how can we figure out which source beliefs are the right ones? How do we know it's *this* belief and not the one inside the next fortune cookie? The usual answer is simple: we choose the beliefs that we *want* to be true. But if we really care about justifying our beliefs, that's hardly enough. We'll have to wrestle with the paradox.

One approach to this challenge is to treat the problem the same way mathematicians approach proofs: they determine a core set of assumptions and then prove theorems based on those assumptions. Instead of presuming source beliefs are beliefs based on faith, let's instead regard them as the starting assumptions for a logical proof. We can put forth a set of core assumptions and then develop a broader system of belief based on those assumptions. If the resulting system fails to create a cohesive and comprehensive system of belief, then we can start over. The initial assumptions can then be reformulated until a set is found that does lead to a consistent, meaningful "theorem of life."

As an example of this process we can look at an age-old question confronted by mapmakers: what is the maximum number of colors needed to color a map so that no two regions—whether countries, counties, or any other shapes—share both a border and a color? In 1852, a student at the University of London named Francis Guthrie took on the challenge while coloring a map of English counties. He realized that, despite the convoluted shapes of some counties and the fact that each shares borders with many other counties, no more than four colors seemed necessary. If he would alternate colors between adjacent neighboring counties he found that he didn't need more than four colors to complete the map. So he made an intuitive assumption that only four colors were sufficient for any map or combination of shapes, real or manufactured, no matter how complex or how arranged. If his assumption were correct, you could throw a handful of cutout shapes on a table—triangles, snowflakes, wavy lines, whatever—and need no more than four colors to color the resulting mess.

The four-color theorem, as it was known, was simple to test but devilishly hard to prove. Generations of mapmakers after Guthrie tested it with every map they made and, sure enough, no one ever needed a fifth color. But this was not the same as proof, of course. There was always the possibility that the next map would need more than four colors. Still, even though the assumption could never be entirely proven by real-world testing, with every successful application of the theorem the odds of such an exception diminished, and confidence in it justifiably increased.

It wasn't until 1976 that a team of mathematicians at the University of Illinois finally harnessed the power of a computer to solve the theorem.[2] (Interestingly, another, more powerful computer was required to test the solution of the first, and that wasn't achieved until 2005.)[3]

Like the four-color theorem, an unproven assumption can be tested to see if it generates a coherent result. The more it does so, the more the confidence in that theorem may increase—even if it is never fully proven.

The approach of treating starting beliefs as assumptions removes the predicament of not knowing how to pick and choose between unjustifiable beliefs. If these beliefs are going to be rudimentary enough to form the basis of any belief system, no other system can be used to pick them because such a system would then become a core belief itself. By adopting the notion of starting assumptions, there's no need to be forced to choose source beliefs. Rather, different combinations of these beliefs can be evaluated in light of the results they yield.

As you will see, the heuristic of this entire book is that we need to be willing to reassess our lives with empirical checks. We need to continuously test our assumptions rather than presuppose them. We must look at everything with fresh eyes and not adopt the biases of others.

TOOLS FOR EVALUATING ASSUMPTIONS

Two other ideas may be useful in selecting a set of starting assumptions. The first is to favor simplicity. This is called Ockham's razor, after the fourteenth-century philosopher and theologian William of Ockham. The "razor" refers to any principle that helps narrow possibilities. This principle states that the answer that requires the fewest assumptions while explaining all of the facts is most likely to be correct.

For example: after taking a stroll one evening, you notice that the lights are on in your apartment. You come up with two possible explanations:

1. You forgot to turn them off when leaving the house.
2. Your neighbor was baking cookies and didn't have milk at home, so he came into your apartment to borrow milk, turned on the lights when he came in, and never turned them off when he left.

The first hypothesis requires only one assumption—that you forgot to turn the lights off. The second hypothesis requires several assumptions—that your neighbor was baking cookies, wanted milk to go with the cookies, didn't have any milk, thought your apartment was the best place to get some, was able to get into your apartment, and left the lights on when he was finished. Both would explain the facts you can see, but if we apply Ockham's razor, we would favor the first hypothesis since it requires fewer assumptions.

If we apply the razor to our search for source beliefs, it follows that a system of beliefs that requires fewer source beliefs has a greater likelihood of being valid. In other words, the fewer leaps of faith (unjustifiable source beliefs) required in order to create a system of belief, the less faith we need and the more confident we can be in the outcome.[4]

Of course, it's possible to misuse this concept—typically by ignoring the requirement to explain all the facts. For example, the hypothesis that height alone determines a person's weight is a lot simpler than the notion that the complex interplay of a few dozen genes, diet, and exercise does so. But the simpler explanation fails to explain all the facts—namely, the stunning range of actual variation we see in real-life height-to-weight ratios. The five-foot-five sumo wrestler who weighs a hundred pounds more than the six-foot-nine basketball player presents an instant (and fatal) problem for the simpler answer. Thus, simpler is better so long as it explains all the facts.

A second tool for choosing basic source beliefs is to think about what it would mean to *deny* a particular source belief. In other words, if a particular belief were not true, would the resulting worldview make sense? To return to the mapmaker's problem, the very first map that required five colors would have rendered the four-color theorem invalid.

There are often logical consequences to accepting or rejecting an assumption, even if it can't be justified with prior assumptions. Evaluating the consequences of beliefs can be helpful in determining what type of assumptions may be needed to form a valid system of belief.

We have to be careful with this tool as well. The best example of its misuse might be the "argument from consequences." God's existence is often assumed to be true because so many people think the consequences of his nonexistence would be terrible.[5]

But you can't argue that something is false solely because it produces consequences that are not *good*. Otherwise you'd have an argument that the Holocaust never happened because the world would be better if it hadn't. On the other hand, you *can* argue that something is false because it produces consequences that are not *true*.

THE MOST BASIC OF ASSUMPTIONS

At this point, our discussion is limited to beliefs about what *facts* we should believe. Later we'll approach the more complex but essential question of how we should *behave*.

We propose that to develop a coherent framework of factual belief, we need to accept three core assumptions:

1. An external reality exists.
2. Our senses perceive this external reality.
3. Language and thought are tools for describing and understanding what our senses perceive.

In the study of philosophy, the belief in the above three assumptions is known as "perspectival realism." These three assumptions are so elemental that we take them for granted in our everyday lives. But it's worth examining them in some depth since they will form the cornerstone of all subsequent beliefs we will discuss.

External Reality

A belief in an external reality is the acceptance that the world, universe, and everything in it physically exist and are real. It is a belief that the world is independent of the way any individual thinks about it.[6] The opposite would be to believe in a mind-created reality, or a reality that resides solely in our minds or our dreams.

It is not possible to definitively *prove* that the world we exist in is indeed an external reality. Reality is perceived only through the perspective of the mind, so the whole thing could just be an illusion.[7] But the reality is that in daily life, we all assume that objects we see actually exist and that our fellow humans can also interact with and perceive them. Anyone who feels uncomfortable with accepting the notion of an external reality should ask why, when leaving a two-story building, he or she would rather walk down the stairs than take a shortcut by just hopping out the window.[8] In *real life*, we don't jump out of windows thinking we'll just float down to the sidewalk unharmed, and we certainly don't behave as if reality were just a figment of our imaginations. Rather, our daily actions show that we take for granted that the world around us is real and that we exist within it.

The existence of an external reality allows for a much greater concept —that "truth" is simply an accurate description of what is. It is our contention that reality and truth *are the same thing*. The world that exists around us right now is a truth. The fact that the air we inhale with each breath consists mostly of nitrogen and oxygen is a truth. The audible words that someone says are a truth. What that person actually means by those words is a truth as well, whether or not others know it. A truth or fact is simply an accurate account of reality. A belief in the contrary—in a subjective view of reality—would deny the existence of facts or certainties. From that perspective, truth becomes a relative concept. My truth—not just my opinions or experience, but my actual truth in apprehension of the universe—could be different from yours.

Consider an example of two friends, both passionate fans of a college basketball team that finished an exciting, record-setting season but lost the conference championship in a squeaker. One claims that the season was a huge success because the team won most of its games and played better than ever before. But the other claims that the season was a failure because they lost the most important game—the championship. Each friend offers differing interpretations of the season, and they even offer different views on what events actually took place in some of the games. But a set of facts exists and is real, whether or not the friends see eye to eye and regardless of their different interpretations—games won and lost, points scored, assists, fouls, the works. The facts happened, even if people differ on what those facts meant.

That is what it means for truth and reality to be one and the same.

Using Our Senses

The second core assumption is that our senses—our eyes, ears, sense of touch, smell, and taste—perceive the external reality around us. Our eyes see a table because a table exists in reality. In theory, this is something we can never prove—that a table really exists or that an object that appears round is truly round. We have no other source of information about whether our perception is accurate.

Bertrand Russell explored the relationship between our senses and reality in his book *The Problems of Philosophy.*[9] We never perceive the world directly, Russell said—we perceive our sense-data, and they in turn perceive the world. The fact that our senses are forever standing between us and reality poses a problem because our senses can be misled by changing conditions or by our state of mind. A table that appears red in the morning can look brown at noon and purple at dusk. It can look huge in a small room and tiny in a cavernous one. Press on the table with your fingertips, and you're not feeling the table—you're feeling the sensation of your fingertips being compressed. Or at least you *think* you are, since any number of things can cause you to experience that sensation. Do you really know that a table is causing that feeling, or is it all in your mind?

Maybe there's no table there at all!

Just about the time Russell has us doubting the existence of tables (and everything else), he rescues reality. Even if a hundred different people describe a given table in a hundred different ways, he reminds us, they can usually agree that they are in fact looking at a table. That common denominator suggests that our confidence in the table's existence is justified, even if we can't quite sort out the details of color, texture, and size. And even if we disagree on everything else, we can accept that it *has* these attributes—it *has* a color, a texture, and a size. And our senses, limited as they are, represent our best chance of discovering the truth about those attributes.

Of course, in everyday life we take for granted the validity of what our senses perceive since we interact with the world all around us. This core assumption further implies that our *only* source for making assessments about what is true or not, what exists in reality and what does not, is our senses. To rephrase, if we can't perceive something or its effects without the use of our senses, then we have no ability to evaluate whether or not it's true.[10]

It goes without saying that the ability of our senses to perceive reality can be greatly enhanced and extended through the use of tools, instruments, and technology. Millions of people see the world around them with better clarity and detail because of their eyeglasses or contact lenses. Scanning electron microscopes let us see tiny objects such as a single hair on the leg of a housefly. Ultrasounds can peer through the womb of a mother to reveal the developmental stage of a fetus. Radar can alert us of aircraft hundreds of miles away. The use of tools and instruments to derive knowledge about the world is commonplace.

But all of these instruments have one crucial thing in common: they all translate their acquired information into a form that we can perceive through our rudimentary senses. It is still our senses alone that ultimately allow us to perceive what these instruments detect. We also rely on our senses to confirm the accuracy of these tools. Looking in the sky for an airplane can validate radar. Looking at the newborn child can confirm the ultrasound diagnosis.

Of course, our senses are not infallible, in part because our minds interpret what we see and can therefore bias our perceptions. Still, aside from people who have mental disorders, what we perceive with our senses is generally accurate. For example, when one looks at a spoon that is placed inside of a glass of water it may appear bent. Although we know that the spoon is not really bent, but refracted, the observation that the spoon *appears* bent is an accurate reflection of what is real. The problem is not with the ability of our senses to observe reality but with the conclusions the mind may draw from what is seen. So if a person thought the spoon actually was bent, that would be a false conclusion based on a misinterpretation of good data. Our senses' abilities to feel the spoon in the water confirm that it is indeed as straight as it was before it went into the glass.

We will deal more with how we should process the information our senses receive and how to deal with conflicting information about what to believe later in the book. At this point it's enough to say our senses are the only source for ascertaining what is real and what is not in the external reality (despite their deficiencies).

The senses we are referring to include only the five rudimentary senses of sight, touch, hearing, smell, and taste.[11] Why not include other senses such as a "sixth sense" (extrasensory perception) or the "heart" (intuition) as part of the list of senses that inform us about what exists in this world? We will deal with this issue more explicitly in forthcoming sections. For now, let's see how much progress can be made by accepting only the five biological senses.

Using Our Minds

The last core assumption we propose is that language and thought are tools for describing and understanding what our senses perceive. The phrase "language and thought" will be used throughout the book to represent a broad range of more nuanced terms, including language, words, semantics, logic, mathematics, statistics, thought, mind, and intellect. This assumption requires us to think about words, definitions, and other concepts in ways that may be unfamiliar. But it is critical for the steps to come, so let's take it slowly and break things down for better comprehension.

Language, words, semantics, logic, mathematics, statistics, thought, mind, the intellect, and the like can be lumped together since they can be viewed as one and the same—tools used to communicate meaning. Such tools create necessary starting points for discourse, and their validity is rooted in their definitions. Consider language for a moment. In order to even ask the question, "How can one justify one's beliefs?" there needs to be agreement on what the words *belief* and *justify* mean.

Agreement is at the heart of language. Unlike physical reality, there's no inherent "truth" about the meaning of a certain word, and there's no universally right word for a given thing or idea. A word means what we mutually agree it means. Reality is independent of our ideas and perceptions of it, but language is entirely dependent on them. There can be many correct words for a single thing (hello, bonjour, guten tag, hola, shalom, néih hóu), and conversely a single sound can mean different things to speakers of different languages. The long i sound, for example, means *eye* in English, *yes* in Scots, and *egg* in German—each the result of subjective agreement in that culture.

For another example of the nature of language, we can turn to the language of mathematics. The Pythagorean theorem asserts that the sum of the squares of the sides of a right-angled triangle equals the square of the hypotenuse. This is true not because there is some inherent wisdom in the assertion but because the definitions of *sum*, *squares*, *equal*, and *triangle* make that statement coherent. It may take the mind of a genius like Pythagoras to demonstrate some of the principles of mathematics, but the proof of the resulting theorem does not require a leap of faith—it just requires an understanding of how we have defined those terms.

These definitional truths can further be used to describe real objects in the external reality—the length of a triangle drawn on paper can represent the measurement of an actual triangular object that exists in the world. Were we not to accept the validity of these tools, we would lack an ability to form any thoughts, concepts, or principles based on what we observe through our senses.

This core assumption in definitional truths also includes the use of our minds and intellect to manipulate and process thoughts and data. The power of our mind allows us to define language and objects, manipulate numbers, and develop rules. By accepting the validity of this assumption, we also accept the use of language and thoughts to derive other facts and information that may not initially be clear to us. We can then use these

conclusions to reflect back on the external reality. This ability to switch between reality and our description of reality allows us to formulate far more
sophisticated concepts and notions than just simple observations. So part of
the acceptance of this assumption means also accepting the ability of our
minds or intellects to organize thoughts, to find links between thoughts,
and to draw conclusions.

THE FIRST THREE NON-COMMANDMENTS

Where does accepting these three basic assumptions really get us? After all,
most of us accept these notions in our everyday lives without feeling the
need to explore all their nuances.

But here's why they are so important: from these three assumptions
alone, it's possible to derive many, many more beliefs. These assumptions
and derived beliefs will help us formulate a framework of beliefs, including
Ten Non-commandments for the Twenty-first Century.

The commonsense nature and seeming simplicity of these assumptions allow us to accept them at a glance. But that very simplicity might be
mystifying. Can these three assumptions really be all we need to justify our
beliefs? Hang on to that question, and we'll see soon enough.

To rephrase the three core assumptions in light of the concepts we
have just discussed, our starting assumptions are:

1. An external reality exists, and "truth" signifies an accurate description of that reality.
2. Our five senses are our only means for perceiving this reality.
3. Language and thought offer ways to analyze, communicate about,
   and contemplate the nature of the reality.

These core assumptions can be summed up as (1) a belief in existence, (2)
an ability to perceive that existence, and (3) instruments for using those
perceptions.

There's still some work to do to determine whether these three core
assumptions are really all we need. For one thing, we need to see what
other beliefs can be derived from these assumptions and test whatever system of belief arises from them. Only when we have a complete, tested system can we be satisfied that our initial assumptions are sufficient. For now,
to keep things moving forward, we only ask that you give us the benefit

of the doubt that the beliefs being proposed will yield a valid outcome. There'll be plenty of time to change your mind if you so choose.

Because these three assumptions are the bedrock beliefs of all subsequent beliefs we will propose, they will serve as the first three non-commandments:

I.   The world is real, and our desire to understand the world is the basis for belief.
II. We can perceive the world only through our human senses.
III. We use rational thought and language as tools for understanding the world.

(For a point-by-point distillation of the concepts presented in this chapter, as well as subsequent chapters throughout the book, we invite you to turn to appendix C, "Theorem of Belief." This appendix summarizes the flow of arguments and the links between the various ideas that are presented. It is the intellectual bones of the book laid bare.)

3

THE REASONING BEHIND REASON

Experience is a hard teacher because she gives the test first, the lesson afterward.

—Vernon Law

What further beliefs can be derived from the three core assumptions? The most significant is the belief in inductive reasoning. To formulate this belief, we can use two of the core assumptions: confidence that our senses reflect reality and acceptance of the language of mathematics.

Inductive reasoning refers to the concept of drawing broad conclusions from specific observations or experiences. Let's look at a simple example. Most of us saw the sun rise today (or at least saw that it had risen).[1] We saw it the day before as well. We have seen it rise on many, many occasions before that. In fact, most of us would have no recollection of a day completely devoid of sunlight. So if we've observed a daily occurrence many times without exception, probability tells us that the chance of it happening again tomorrow is extremely high. In other words, it's reasonable for us to expect that the sun will rise again tomorrow.

Of course, as philosopher David Hume pointed out almost three centuries ago, a reasonable expectation isn't the same as certainty. Despite a track record of more than a million consecutive sunrises in recorded human history, there's no way we can be absolutely certain the sun will rise tomorrow. Many a chicken waddles around day after day feeling confident—cocky, you might say—that it will waddle again tomorrow. But little does the chicken know that tomorrow may bring plucked feathers and a farmer's cooking pot.[2] So, no, we can't be sure about the sunrise. What we *can* say is that based on our previous experiences, the chance that the sun will rise tomorrow is extremely probable, even if we understand that someday the sun will implode and go supernova—putting a definitive end to sunrises on Earth.

CONFIDENCE IN BELIEFS

Since beliefs are derived from prior beliefs, statistically speaking, a derived belief necessarily has less credibility than the belief it's derived from. Conversely, the closer a derived belief is to a source belief, the more credibility we can give it, and the greater confidence we can place in such a belief. For example, we can believe things confirmed by our senses more readily than things only confirmed by the observations of others. That's why "I'll believe it when I see it" is one of our oldest statements of skepticism.

The use of the phrase "confidence in a belief" may seem odd, since most people intuitively think that you either believe a proposition or you reject it. It's a fact or it's not. After all, didn't we just argue that an external reality exists? While the truth is an absolute, our ability to assess that truth is not. We're all fallible beings with different observations and experiences, and we can't be sure about the complete validity of each belief. We can use statistics to help decide how much confidence we should have in each belief, attaching a probability to each belief to capture the degree of our uncertainty.[3]

To get a better idea of how assigning probabilities to beliefs can work, let's return to the sunrise. Isn't our belief that the sun will rise tomorrow also based on the absence of any reports by any person—ever—of the sun failing to rise? Isn't it also based on Newton's theory of gravity and Kepler's laws of planetary motion? All of these complement our belief that the sun will rise tomorrow, so we can add them to our own observations to drive the probability even higher. We can also note that inductive reasoning (reasoning that seeks evidence to increase confidence in a conclusion) is at the heart of each one of these beliefs.

Let's take a look at each of these sunrise confidence boosters.

We'll begin with the testimony of others throughout history who have seen the sun rise without fail. To decide whether or not to believe a particular source, we can evaluate whether or not that source has generally told the truth in the past. A belief in inductive reasoning gives us confidence that someone who has been an accurate source in the past is likely to be an accurate source on similar matters in the future.

We all have years of experience evaluating which sources of second-hand testimony are reliable, so we naturally keep a mental list of sources that we trust as well as those we do not. So, if we need to know what happened in the Franco-Prussian War, we'll put more confidence in textbooks and peer-reviewed published articles than the opinion of Aunt Mildred. That doesn't mean the publications are perfect or that Aunt Mildred is a pathological liar. It just means our experience leads us to expect more reliable information on *that kind of topic* from the former than from the latter. If the topic was Uncle Jack's snoring, Aunt Mildred would be the more reliable source.

That leads to a follow-up question: should you put more confidence in your own beliefs or in the beliefs of other people? Does the fact that you've seen the sun rise so many times outweigh historical records testifying to the same thing?

It's an interesting question. When assessing someone else's testimony, especially over the span of years, you have to accept more links in a chain of beliefs than with your own observations. In general, the closer a belief is to a core assumption, the greater statistical credibility it has. That's because the closer it is to a bedrock assumption, the more likely it's true. Believing in one's own observations only requires a belief in one's own inductive reasoning, but believing in the testimony of others requires believing that they really saw the event *and* are giving an accurate account. A detective will tell you that eyewitness testimony is often as varied as the number of observers. The Innocence Project reports that nearly three out of four convictions that are eventually overturned by DNA testing included eyewitness misidentification.[4]

The statistics can get far more confusing. Imagine a thirty-year-old woman named Caroline who lives in California. Caroline will have consciously seen the sun rise for about ten thousand days in a row. Statistically, based on Caroline's personal observations alone, the probability that the sun will *not* rise tomorrow is about 1 in 10,001. But what if we accept instead the collective testimony of everyone who has lived in the last two thousand years? Suddenly, the chance the sun will not rise tomorrow is about 1 in 500 trillion.[5] So even if Caroline decides to attribute less weight to the testimony of others, the incredible consistency of their data in this case lends enormous weight to her own observations.

To generalize a little more: to determine how much credibility we can attribute to things we've *personally* observed, compared to those observed by others, we can simply assign greater credibility to the source that has historically been more accurate in predicting future events. If Caroline sees that her own inductive conclusions are usually less accurate than those she learns from others, she can decide to lend more weight to their predictions than her own.

This leads to a surprising conclusion. Although one of the assumptions (the first non-commandment) is that there is an external reality or truth, how much each individual believes in a particular aspect of that reality isn't truly objective—it's based on the experiences that he or she has had in life. While the moon's existence is certainly regarded as a fact, it would seem appropriate for a blind person to have less confidence in the moon's existence than in the existence of sounds.

Let's take a less extreme example. You might be more likely to believe that smoking can be bad for a person's health if you have personally witnessed the decline in the health of your chain-smoking grandfather. It also follows that your beliefs can and should change over time as you experience different things or come across compelling data that contradict your existing beliefs.

THE USE OF SCIENCE

The concept that our experiences and perspectives are central to how we form beliefs about the world is called *perspectival realism*. It says that an observer can never be completely objective since this would require a view external to any one perspective—or what philosopher Thomas Nagel famously called "the view from nowhere."[6] Given the fallibility of our senses, the best view we can manage is the view from multiple sources and perspectives. Then we can compare those different models of reality and combine different pieces of reliable perspective to form a more holistic and accurate view of reality. You may recognize this as the very method we discussed in chapter 2, quoting philosopher Bertrand Russell. He decided that even if reports vary regarding the color and size of a table, the fact that everyone sees a table gives him enough confidence in its existence to set a casserole on it.

We'll never see the exact truth about any aspect of the world, because we are limited by our perspectives. However, our observations and inductive reasoning can still lead us to good approximations of the truth. In order to describe the way we form our conceptions of reality, philosopher Ron Giere suggested that human beings intrinsically create a mental model or "map" of reality.[7] A good map doesn't claim a one-to-one relationship between itself and reality. A map always has less detail than is available in the real world. But the stronger the correspondence between the map and reality, the better we consider the map. Trying on several perspectives improves the detail of our mental maps of reality.

How relevant is the scientific use of laws and equations to describe the fact that the sun will rise tomorrow? Inductive reasoning is the foundation of the scientific method. So is careful use of observational data (our senses) and use of language and mathematics (definitional truths). The scientific method is a way to gain knowledge by making observations and doing experiments to validate that knowledge. It can be summarized as a process with five steps:[8]

1. Make observations about the world.
2. Construct a hypothesis that could explain the observations.
3. Test the hypothesis through observable, empirical, and measurable experiments.
4. Analyze the data, and draw a conclusion on the validity or invalidity of the hypothesis.
5. Communicate the data and results with others for criticism or concurrence.

This method is both simple and powerful. Suppose you grow tomatoes in your backyard, and you've noticed that some vines grow bigger, better tomatoes than others. There's the observation. You guess that the plants getting more water are doing better. There's your hypothesis. You test this by carefully watering each vine in the row with a different, premeasured amount of water every day for a full season. At the end of the season, you record the number and sizes of the tomatoes and learn, to your surprise, that the tomatoes at the end of the row, the ones that received the *least* water each day, actually did the best.

But before you start watering all of your tomatoes with an eyedropper, you take that crucial fifth step—sharing your data with others who have a more objective view. That's when someone notices a flaw in your study design: the tomatoes you watered least were also at the downhill end of the row. They weren't getting much water from you. But, thanks to gravity, they were getting a daily sip from their uphill neighbors.

So it's back to the drawing board to test with level rows. That's how science works.

The scientific method is a great ally to the current framework of belief because it systematizes the process for inductive reasoning. It allows us to be confident in millions of discoveries and observations made with the use of that method. The discovery of bacteria and the dawn of modern health care, the discovery of the role of DNA in reproduction and genetic traits, the understanding of electricity, and the advent of the microchip and personal computer—these are just a few examples of human achievement made possible by this careful, systematic, peer-reviewed means of interrogating the world.

But for all its power and achievement, the question remains: is the scientific method the right tool for predicting whether the sun will rise tomorrow?

The answer is a definite yes. The scientific description of the orbit of the earth around the sun is just a much better attempt at describing the situation than our own inductive conclusions. And, unlike our intuition that the sun goes around the earth, the scientific description has the advantage of being demonstrably correct. Science tells us how and when the sun will rise tomorrow and enables us to predict what time it will be in a particular location in the sky.

Even so, science is not very good at telling us *why* the sun will rise. Gravity has been well described, but the exact reason that objects with mass attract each other is still a bit of a puzzle. There are theories, but without corroborating observations and consensus among scientists, it's reasonable to place much less confidence in the explanations provided by these theories than in the simple description of the motion of celestial bodies that has been tested and validated now for four hundred years.

It's also worth mentioning that conventional science sometimes turns out to be not strictly wrong but incomplete. That was the case when Newtonian gravity was amended by Einstein's general relativity. That's why the strength of any belief should be proportional to the evidence and to the knowledge and intellectual abilities of those people articulating that belief. Beliefs can and should be reevaluated as new evidence or information is available. Newton put forth the simplest explanation that was consistent with the data he had observed at the time. New data became available later, so a more complete description was necessary. Beliefs that change or become discredited do not invalidate the scientific method or inductive reasoning. They capture the fact that we don't always have perfect information, so a probabilistic method is the most appropriate way to capture the uncertainty inherent in any belief.

While science is generally a reliable way to know about the world, the people practicing science—*scientists*—are also fallible human beings. They make errors and are plagued by the same desires for money, power, and influence as others. These influences sometimes taint the quality of their research. Consider, for example, the researcher from the University of Vermont College of Medicine who falsified data about therapies for menopause in order to receive several federal research grants totaling $2.9 million.[9] Having confidence in the scientific method doesn't mean that scientific research and data are beyond reproach. In fact, one of the great strengths of the method is that fifth step, the requirement to communicate findings and invite criticism by those outside of a given scientist's biases. Scientific careers are made by invalidating findings just as they are made by validating them. The collective desire for accuracy serves as a powerful check on the individual desire to be right. That's how the researcher's errant data were uncovered and corrected. As a result, he was prosecuted and sentenced to one year of jail time in federal prison. By cross-validating results, challenging results, and debating competing theories, the best science emerges over time.

COLLATING DATA

Where does understanding or intelligence fit into the picture? It is possible to think of examples where inductive reasoning would seem to lead to false conclusions. For example, let's go back to the sun. Instead of Caroline the Californian, let's turn to Albert the Alaskan. He's seen a lot of sunrises too, of course. But in Barrow, Alaska, Albert's hometown, the tilt of the earth means that in winter the sun doesn't rise every day. Does inductive reasoning mean that because Albert has seen the sun rise for so many days, he should always expect it to rise on another given day? Of course not. In this case, his understanding of physics and his awareness that the sun doesn't rise at all in northern Alaska in midwinter will trump the simple inductive conclusion that the sun rises every day.

But that example doesn't mean we have to throw inductive reasoning away in favor of some completely new way of thinking. Albert's improved understanding is just the result of using other observations and inductive reasoning, combining and weighting them to form beliefs that become more complex than simple observational data. It's just inductive reasoning played forward.

Growing up in Barrow, it might have been reasonable at first for little boy Albert to believe the sun would rise every day. But as he grew, he would have started putting the pieces together. He might have noticed that the days got dramatically shorter in the months before the sun disappeared entirely. These observations would lead him to form other inductive beliefs that could recognize patterns in when the sun would indeed rise and how long it would shine each day. As he went through high school, he would have learned how physics and astronomy predict the motion of the earth around the sun and the times and durations of sun exposure around the world. His belief in the validity of the concepts taught to him at school would have been solidified by other inductive observations about the soundness of the information his science teachers taught him. In the end, an "understanding" of why the sun rises or doesn't rise could override Albert's simplistic direct observations. This wouldn't contradict his inductive reasoning ability—it would be the product of multiple steps of inductive reasoning.

THE FOURTH NON-COMMANDMENT

From our three core assumptions, we were able to gain confidence in inductive reasoning. With induction, we can generate many other beliefs based on observations and experiences in life. The scientific method is an effective tool for discerning facts and, just as importantly, for learning what previous knowledge is no longer accurate. A critical part of that method is the control of our biases in the service of an accurate view of reality. Certain beliefs can be held more strongly than others. The basis for deciding how strongly to hold a belief should be the evidence encountered along the way, as well as the odds that the evidence is correct. Conflicting beliefs can be resolved by deciding which belief has the greater likelihood of being true, based on the evidence.

In summary, we've formulated a belief that inductive reasoning and the scientific method are tools for establishing the truth. The key principle in both is the notion that the strength of a belief is tied to the evidence in its support.

Let's see where we are when we add this conclusion to our Ten Non-commandments:

I.   The world is real, and our desire to understand the world is the basis for belief.
II. We can perceive the world only through our human senses.
III. We use rational thought and language as tools for understanding the world.
IV. *All truth is proportional to the evidence.*

4

BELIEFS ABOUT THE UNKNOWN

Make everything as simple as possible, but not simpler.

—Albert Einstein

While inductive reasoning takes advantage of observations and evidence, it's sometimes necessary to form beliefs when observation and evidence are not available. "Is there life after death?" and "Do we have a soul?" are just two examples. How can we approach questions like these?

When experience is limited, a process such as favoring simplicity (Ockham's razor) becomes especially powerful. It lets us generalize the belief that the explanation of the facts requiring the fewest assumptions is probably the right one. Put another way, if you have two possible explanations, and they both explain the data, the simpler one is usually right.

So let's put Ockham's razor to work on beliefs that cannot be underpinned by observation and evidence.

That middle phrase above—"and they both explain the data"—is key. Favoring simplicity doesn't just mean "simpler is better." To be in the running at all, an explanation has to fit all of the facts. Simpler is better only if the simpler explanation also completely *works*. Favoring simplicity suggests that we should tend toward simpler explanations until we can trade some simplicity for the increased explanatory power of the facts. Isaac Newton captured this well when he said, "We are to admit no more causes of natural things than such as are both true and sufficient to explain their appearances."[1]

Since this principle of favoring simplicity is not itself a core assumption, just a guide in formulating the assumptions, we still have one major obstacle to overcome. This principle needs to be logically deduced so that the overall framework remains coherent. The good news is that favoring simplicity—also known as the "principle of parsimony"—can be validated not only through personal experiences, but also by figuring out probabilities for alternate theories.

The simplest kind of theory includes just one principle, while more complex theories rely on more than one. Since each principle attached to a theory is a form of belief, each belief includes a probability that the belief is accurate. The more you multiply probabilities in a single function, the smaller the probability of the function becomes. In other words, assuming all things being the same between two different theories, the more principles on which a theory relies, the lower the probability that it will be true.

Suppose we're all sitting, bored, on a small-town street corner one afternoon and decide to pass the time by betting on the next car to go by. If one of us said, "I'll bet you five bucks that the next car that goes by will be white," you might not take that bet. You know that white is a very popular car color, so you could very well end up losing five bucks.

If one of us said, "I'll bet the next car that goes by will be a Ford," you're probably not going to take that bet either. Half the cars in small-town America are Fords. But if one of us said, "I'll bet the next car that goes by will be a white 1969 Ford Mustang convertible," you'll most likely jump on that bet in a heartbeat. Each one of those five principles (white, 1969, Ford, Mustang, convertible) lowers the probability of the next car being a match. Put them all together, and you're about to be five dollars richer.

To see why, let's take a look at how the probabilities stack up. Let's say we assume (generously) that each one of these "principles" is equally likely, and each has a 50 percent likelihood of being true. So the odds of the following events are each 50 percent probable: the next car is white; it's from the 1969 model year; it's a Ford; it's a Mustang; and it's a convertible.

These are insanely generous odds, of course—for example, the assumption that half the cars on the road are from 1969. To calculate the overall likelihood of winning the bet, we multiply the individual probabilities of each event together. We multiply the chance that the car is white (50 percent) by the chances it's a 1969 (50 percent) and a Ford (50 percent) and a Mustang (50 percent) and a convertible (50 percent) . . . which yields a combined probability of just 3.125 percent (50 percent × 50 percent × 50 percent × 50 percent × 50 percent). So even in this dream world saturated with classic Mustangs, the chance of winning this bet is still incredibly small.

The above example shows that increasing the number of variables in an explanation reduces the overall likelihood of the explanation being correct, even if the variables are all equally likely.

Variables aren't always equally likely, of course, and so the probabilities should be factored in. If you have an explanation with three very probable principles, it's more likely to be true than one with two improbable principles—and we should always favor the explanation that's most probable. But all other things being equal, increasing complexity should reduce our confidence. Simpler is better, so long as it fully describes the facts.

All this suggests that favoring simplicity isn't a law or a foolproof principle. Rather, it's a tool for deciding between competing ideas when there's not much helpful evidence. As you'll see, the questions we'll be analyzing in this chapter are of exactly that kind.

IN THE WHITE ROOM

Let's start with a thought experiment. A woman in a white lab coat is about to ask you a series of questions about what exists or doesn't exist, and you are required to answer them. For every right answer, she will give you a hundred dollars. You pride yourself on being a rational thinker who analyzes the reasons for your choices, so you're already thinking about the new iPad you plan to buy with the money.

The examiner blindfolds you, places you in a windowless van, and drives you off to an unknown location. When the blindfold is finally removed, you find yourself sitting in a white room. The only furniture are two plain stainless steel chairs. You are sitting on one, the examiner on the other. In the corner of the room there is a mysterious, bright-orange sphere that appears to be floating magically in the air. The examiner informs you that you are not to move from your chair or explore your surroundings. She then proceeds to ask you the following questions:

1. Is this room located in a larger building?
2. Is the structure you are in next door to a bank?
3. Is the mysterious sphere in the corner being held up by a newly discovered physical phenomenon?
4. Is the mysterious ball being held up by an invisible table?

Okay, four questions, you think, none of them with obvious answers, so goodbye new iPad. Still, the questions present an interesting challenge . . . and you still want to get the most money you can.

How should you answer those four questions? The most appropriate answer to all of them is, "I don't know." After all, you are in a foreign environment with an unexplained sphere in the corner. How can you claim to have any real knowledge to help answer those questions?

On the other hand, "I don't know" also means no cash, so you buckle down and force yourself to make decisions that have the highest probability of being correct.

Okay, you decide, *let's try the first question:* "Is this room located in a larger building?" Obviously, you have no way of knowing for sure if the room is a single isolated box in the middle of a deserted parking lot or whether it is one room in a twenty-story building. But even though you don't have any direct evidence to help you decide, you still aren't completely lost. For one thing, "rooms" are not a completely alien concept to you.

So you ponder. *I've never seen this particular room before, nor any bare white room with such sparse furniture. But I've entered many other rooms of different sizes in my life, some about this size. So even without direct evidence for what's outside of this room, my general experience with life is helpful. Most of the rooms I've entered were part of some larger building structure. So using probability and inductive reasoning, I can say that the odds that this is a single isolated room are very low.* "Yes," you tell the examiner, "this room is part of a larger building."

Next question. "Is the structure you are in next door to a bank?" Again, you have no direct evidence, but you can still draw upon information from related experiences in your life. *There are many uses for buildings,* you tell yourself, *and if I were to ask myself if the building next door was a bank on random occasions, the answer would almost always be no.* "No," you tell her, "the building next door is not a bank."

The examiner's face gives nothing away. "Is the mysterious sphere in the corner of the room held up by a newly discovered physical phenomenon?" *Well, I have very little experience with anything like this ball. How can I explain it? It could indeed be a new phenomenon, or it could be some type of a magician's illusion, like a magnetically levitated ball, a hologram, or the Pepper's Ghost² effect. Which is most likely? Since I have no experience or direct evidence, I'll favor simplicity and choose the one that requires the least reevaluation of what I already know.* So you follow your first impulse that it is most likely an optical illusion. You tell the examiner, "The ball is not held up by a new physical phenomenon."

Final question: "Is the mysterious ball being held up by an invisible, undetectable table?" *Okay,* you tell yourself, *this is a different kind of dilemma. If the table is invisible and undetectable, it would logically satisfy what I'm observing: an orange sphere that appears to float in midair. But to believe this, I'd also have to believe in the existence of invisible tables, something I've never before encountered.*

The good news is that you have two principles now to help you make your decision. The first is that not believing in invisible tables would be a simpler solution than believing in them. The second and more important is that if the object holding up the ball is undetectable, how do you know it's a table? After all, couldn't an invisible shelf, an invisible box, or an invisible chair be holding it up? Those are no less likely than an invisible table.

So you answer, "The ball is not held up by an invisible table."

The result? You walk away with three hundred dollars. It turns out that the room is one of many in a television studio building. The ball in the corner turns out to be held in position by a very thin rod that extends out from the far wall, so you can't see it. But the building does happen to be next to a Wells Fargo bank. Such is life.

INDIRECT EVIDENCE

The previous scenario offers a powerful method for dealing with situations in which we're forced to make choices about what we believe without any direct evidence for or against a position. In such cases, we can only rely on indirect evidence.

The two questions that dealt with the room were different from the ones that dealt with the mysterious orange ball. Those first two questions do not cast any doubt on your preexisting view of the world. They merely ask you to make a conjecture about things you haven't experienced by reflecting on things you have.

To do this, you rely on related experiences in your own life—that most rooms you've ever entered have been part of a larger building and that most buildings are not banks. The "bank" question emphasizes a principle that we will refer to as the "folly of the lottery ticket." For example, let's say you buy a Mega Millions lottery ticket from the California state lottery. Your chances of winning the jackpot are one in 176,000,000.[3] You are asked if you believe that your ticket will win and told you must answer yes or no. You have no way of determining whether or not this random ticket is the winner, so it is foolish to believe that you are holding the winning ticket. You may *hope* it's the winning ticket, but if you *believe* it's the winner and start spending all that money, you'll quickly wish you hadn't. Sound judgment argues that it's not a winning lottery ticket, for the laws of probability predict that this belief would be correct almost 100 percent of the time.

A key concept here is that you can't tell what a winning ticket looks like until the results are announced. Each lottery ticket can have many characteristics: one could be dirty, another might have a torn edge, another might be creased, the numbers on one could all be odd, and another even—but none of these characteristics have any meaningful connection to the likelihood of that ticket being a winner. So to believe with any kind of certainty that yours is the winning ticket is to fall into the "folly of the lottery ticket."

By the same token, to believe that the neighboring building to the white room is a bank is unsound, since it requires believing in one specific outcome out of many equally plausible ones. Sitting in that white room, you have no way of distinguishing why a bank is any more likely to be located outside the building than a grocery store, a hair salon, or a restaurant—especially since there are many more popular retail buildings than banks. In fact, even after you learn that you are wrong in this case, you still realize that you made the best guess.

In this scenario, you were forced to choose "yes" or "no" when you would prefer to reply, "I don't know." Life often forces us to take a position on matters where we may not precisely *know* what to believe but must choose anyway.

The questions about the orange ball force you to deal with something that you have never directly encountered before and something that directly conflicts with the way you expect the world to behave—namely, that objects do not float in air.

How can we bridge the gap between what we have experienced and a particular event that contradicts our expectations? Favoring simplicity means our current knowledge should be favored over inventing or creating new phenomena to explain inconsistencies or puzzles.

The "invisible table" question highlights the point that while some solutions may appear to be logically consistent—an invisible table *would* explain it, after all—creating a whole new phenomenon makes little sense if other explanations are available within the bounds of what we already know. And since we can't acquire any specific information about the object, believing it is a table instead of a shelf invokes the "folly of the lottery ticket." If the ball could be held up by an invisible table, couldn't it be held up by an invisible box or an invisible chair? What about an invisible genie, or an invisible monster, an invisible fairy . . .

. . . or God?

If no experience can validate one explanation over another, all explanations are equally likely (or unlikely). The chance that the explanation you picked on that second question in the white room is correct is unimaginably small since you're picking one choice from an infinite number of potential choices—every one of them as undetectable as the winning lottery ticket before the draw.

You'll recall that we arrived at a fourth non-commandment in the last chapter: all truth is proportional to the evidence. This statement already embodies the concept of favoring simplicity and the problem of the "folly of the lottery ticket." We favor simplicity because simpler evidence tends to produce more accurate predictions. With the lottery ticket scenario, all tickets are equally unlikely to be the winner, *even the actual winner*, because no evidence can be produced in advance to favor picking one ticket over another.

Since the fourth non-commandment already captures what was explored in this chapter, we will not add anything additional to the list of non-commandments. But the concepts we explored in this chapter will be very useful in the chapters to come.

To recap the list of non-commandments so far:

I. The world is real, and our desire to understand the world is the basis for belief.
II. We can perceive the world only through our human senses.
III. We use rational thought and language as tools for understanding the world.
IV. All truth is proportional to the evidence.

Now, let's tackle the question of God.

5

THE ASSUMPTION OF A GOD

We are all atheists about most of the gods that humanity has ever believed in. Some of us just go one god further.

—Richard Dawkins

The first four non-commandments dealt with beliefs about existence— that is, what is true and real in the universe. The remaining non-commandments will deal with human behavior and ethics.

But before we begin discussing ethics, we need to explore a particular belief that relates to existence—the existence of a God. If this sounds more like an afterthought than the next logical step in our process, it is because, for a nonbeliever, that is exactly what we are doing; we are clearing away one final remnant that—given the view of the world we have already discussed—is no longer tenable.

Many people see a central role for God and religion in influencing human behavior and morality. So before we dig into ethics, we need to tackle once and for all the question of whether God exists. As it turns out, that strange scenario about rooms, banks, and glowing orange balls in the last chapter is very useful in answering this question.

That's because it gives us a reference for how we might answer questions on a topic when we don't have much direct knowledge or experience.

Let's ask the same questions we were asked in that room, only this time about a Supreme Being. Take the question about whether the room was in a larger building. This is a question about scale and number. A similar question related to God is this:

Is there one God, or more than one?

Whether the room was next to a bank is a question about specificity of type. A similar question related to God would be:

Is God the Christian God?

The question of whether the ball was held up by a new phenomenon is a question about the supernatural. A similar question would be:

Does God supersede the laws of nature?

The question of whether the ball is held up by an invisible table is a question about attributes. Similar questions about God include:

Is God a completely just God?

Is God omniscient, omnipotent, and omni-benevolent?[1]

All of these questions about God have a common characteristic: they all assume from the start that a God or gods exist. None of the questions allow for the possibility that God isn't real to begin with. Rather, they start by assuming the existence of God and then quickly move on to asking questions about what *type* of God exists.

Let's try to answer those questions as well as we can, presuming for now that God exists. That will better position us later on to answer the question of whether or not God does indeed exist, because we'll better understand the attributes and characteristics of God.

IS THERE A SINGLE GOD, OR ARE THERE MULTIPLE GODS?

Polytheism is less common in modern times, but many great cultures throughout history have believed in polytheism, including the ancient Egyptians, Greeks, and Romans.

When you answered the question about whether the room was located in a larger building, you said "yes," because most of the rooms you've encountered have been in larger buildings. Applying the same principle to the belief in God is more difficult. Unlike rooms, most people would say they haven't had a personal experience with a God or gods before. Assuming you are among them, how can you determine whether there is one God or multiple gods?

Well, one thing you can do is to focus instead on one attribute of God with which you do have experience and make an educated guess by extrapolating from that attribute.

For example, you can focus on God's attribute of being the creator of the world and universe. No doubt you encounter numerous objects each day that were invented in your lifetime: laptop computers, the Internet, Hot Pockets, e-books, ballpoint pens . . .

A few of these inventions were no doubt the creation of a solitary genius. But, more likely, especially in the modern world, they were the product of collaborations. A survey of the United States Patent Office, a very large database for inventions, quickly shows that the vast majority of inventions have multiple people listed as contributing to their creation.

Consider one particularly well-known invention: the Apple iPhone. Apple has 416 patents related to the iPhone alone.[2] One of them, U.S. Patent 7,479,949 (touch screen device, method, and graphical user interface for determining commands by applying heuristics), deals only with the aspect of the iPhone that relates to multitouch functionality—and that patent alone lists twenty-five different inventors. As this example illustrates, inventions—and particularly complex ones—tend to take the efforts of many to bring to fruition.

If we were to apply this same characteristic to the question of whether there is a single God creator or multiple god creators, based only on our experience with inventions, we probably would come down on the side of multiple gods. After all, the iPhone is a complex device, but it's much less complex than the universe.

IS GOD THE CHRISTIAN GOD?

When you answered the question about whether the room was next door to a bank, your response was "no" because it was far more likely to be next to something else—a home, a retail store, or any of a thousand other possibilities. This choice seems obvious, because banks make up only a tiny fraction of the possible options. Applying the same methodology to the question of which type of God might exist, you have many choices. Jews believe in one type of God. Muslims believe in another. So too do Hindus, Mormons, Sikhs, and Christians. If we count historical gods as well, the number grows exponentially. To name a few examples, you would have to count Greek gods (Zeus, Hermes, Hades, Hera, Aphrodite, Dionysus), Norse gods (Othin, Thor, Loki, Njord), Egyptian gods (Ba, Isis, Anubis, Osiris), Sumerian gods (An, Ki, Enlil, Enki), Aboriginal gods (Baiame, Wuriupranili, Yhi)—the list goes on and on. Well over 2,500 deities have been catalogued by historians.[3] As a matter of fact, depending on how you define "god," Hinduism alone is said to have as many as 330 million of them.[4]

Which defining characteristics should you use to guess well about which God or gods are most likely to exist?

That's a tough one. Was Jesus more accurate in predicting the way the world works than Allah? Is the God described in the Book of Mormon wiser than the God of the Torah? This dilemma is a lot like the lottery ticket problem. As we've already discussed, when you look at two lottery tickets before the draw, you have no way to tell which one is the winner, or even if they are both losers.

The same is true of gods: put one next to another, and there's no way to tell which is more likely to be real.[5] Any choice among the various gods is arbitrary, because you have no way of knowing which one is holding the winning ticket. And that means you have to conclude that God is not the Christian God, because putting your money on any given number of a roulette wheel with 2,500 numbers (or more) would be a terrible bet statistically.[6] And even if you were to decide to believe in the Christian God, you'd still need to choose among the various versions described by the 41,000 different sects of Christianity.[7] And how would you decide between the Catholic version of God, the Calvinist version, the Pentecostal, the Seventh-day Adventist, and so on?

What if instead of asking whether God is a Christian God, the question were changed to, *Which version of God is most likely correct?*

A good way to start is to admit to not having the requisite skills to assess the track records of the various gods' predictions. That means you will need to rely on the experience of others who seem to have those skills. You are also more likely to trust the people closest to you because, as far as you can tell, they have never tried to deliberately deceive you. Given that, you are most likely to end up believing in the God in which your parents and family members believe.

If your parents are Jewish, you'll likely pick the Jewish God. If your brothers are Mormons, you'll likely go with the Mormon God. Still, you owe it to yourself to at least consider the testimony of the vast number of believers in other major religions. And as you look around, it appears that believers in the God of Jesus make up a greater number than any other single option.[8]

Is it the God of Moses or the God of Jesus? Your decision comes down to this: shall you ascribe greater weight to the wisdom of those closest to you or to that held by the greatest number of strangers? If you are like most people, you'll pick the God of your ancestors.

DOES GOD HAVE THE POWER
TO SUPERSEDE THE LAWS OF NATURE?

When you were asked if the orange ball was held up by some new phenomenon, you answered "no" because it was simpler (Ockham's razor) to believe that you were witnessing an optical illusion than some new physical phenomenon you'd never before encountered, specifically for levitating orange balls.

Let's apply the same process to the question of a God: would it be simpler for you to believe that nature is constant and unchanging . . . or that God alters the laws of nature?

The Bible describes many times when God intervened and manipulated the laws of nature with miracles. God created a fire in a bush that was never consumed.[9] God stopped the sun in the sky for Joshua to battle.[10] Moses parted the Red Sea.[11] Jesus walked on water[12] and raised the dead.[13] By applying Ockham's razor, it's pretty easy to decide that the likelihood of these miracles having really occurred (as opposed to misreporting, confusion, or hysteria) is very low—especially given that you have not heard of any similar miracles in the modern era. You can only conclude that God, and especially today's God, does not operate outside the laws of nature.

But wait a minute. What of those modern-day claimed miracles, such as accounts of patients recovering from a terminal illness or infertile couples unexpectedly becoming parents? Should you ascribe these "miracles" to acts of God or, rather, to our misunderstanding of nature? It seems a whole lot simpler to believe that such events are not the work of God or gods but rather are rare outlier events that occur very infrequently, are errors in diagnosis, or push the limits of medical understanding. If you are not yet comfortable favoring simplicity and the laws of nature over a belief in miracles, see appendix A, "Common Religious Objections," where we discuss miracles in greater depth.

IS GOD OMNISCIENT,
OMNIPOTENT, AND OMNI-BENEVOLENT?

When answering whether the orange ball was held up by an invisible, undetectable table, you concluded it was not. That's because, according to the folly of the lottery ticket, to believe that a table is holding up the ball (instead of a shelf, box, chair, or the like) would be to pick one attribute out of many equally plausible invisible attributes.

Applying this same principle to the attributes of God, you would reject the notion that God is a completely just god because the potential for God to be unjust, moderately just, minimally just, or even occasionally just would be at least equally plausible alternatives. If we have no way of evaluating the justness of God (and at least as much apparent evidence for injustice as justice), picking that specific choice out of many possibilities would be a terrible bet.

By the same logic, you can't confidently bet that God is all-powerful or eternal, because either of those choices would be betting on a single attribute from many alternatives.

Where does that leave us? Combining the answers from the above questions, you might conclude that:

- It's more plausible that many gods exist.
- Those gods have the disposition of the gods your family has historically believed in.
- Those gods hold no special powers above the laws of nature.
- Those gods are not completely just.

Now, we'll admit that presenting the above conclusions has been somewhat tongue-in-cheek on our part, for they show that even if you assume the existence of a God, defining the attributes of such a God presents some insurmountable challenges. Meanwhile, if you answer questions about the characteristics of God on their own merits and apply the same principles we use in our everyday lives in situations where we have limited information, and you don't presuppose a particular religious view, you end up with some pretty strange notions of what that God might be like.

It would seem that believers in God don't just believe in God; they also assume a lot of other things about the nature of God.

Now that we've made this one last attempt at figuring out what God might be like, we can ask a more fundamental question.

DOES GOD EXIST AT ALL?

Since this is a question about existence, we can use the framework of belief we've already elaborated in the previous chapters. When we do that, we can see that a belief in God is inconsistent with the system of belief we've already proposed.

Why? For two principal reasons.

1. No Observable Evidence

Since the qualities, powers, and workings of God are supernatural, we have no way to directly observe any attributes of God that would allow us to form reliable beliefs about his existence or nonexistence.

Remember that one of our core assumptions (the second noncommandment) is that our senses are all we have for figuring out the nature of reality. And since none of God's characteristics are observable, God can't be identified as belonging to the external reality. Simply put, there is no observable evidence to corroborate a belief in the existence of a God.

At the same time, favoring simplicity helps us dismiss the notion of the supernatural altogether, since there are much simpler explanations for describing the laws of nature than the work of an unseen deity. It's much simpler to explain wind as the flow of air across thermal gradients than as the actions of invisible, supernatural gods. It's also simpler to explain earthquakes by the natural, explicable movements of tectonic plates than by the actions of invisible, supernatural gods. And as Ockham's razor has demonstrated time and time again, the simpler explanation is usually the right one.

2. The Religious Lottery

The second reason we can dismiss the notion of God's existence comes from the "folly of the lottery ticket." We have no way to intelligently choose among the many forms of God and the various religions. So the likelihood that the god of one's parents turns out to be the right one out of so many options—well, the probability of that being the case is just insignificantly small.

But let's be honest. While we can debate forever the merits of how to justify a belief in God, the real reason people tend to believe in God is not because of the existence of corroborating evidence or because of logical reasons for such belief. No, people believe in God out of *faith*. Or, to put it into the terms we've been using, people believe in a given religion because they choose it as their set of starting assumptions. A religion is assumed to be true, and only then does a whole system of belief and behavior emerge from that assumption.

In short, God is an *assumption*, not a belief.

Remember, we've already shown that starting assumptions are never logically justifiable. Right? Otherwise they aren't starting assumptions. But in real life we operate from them anyway. So why are religious assumptions any less valid than an assumption about an objective reality? We can't logically *prove* that any assumption has more or less merit than any other. But we can say that the assumptions we've already made lead us to a system that doesn't need God to function successfully.

Worse still, the God assumption conflicts directly with the beliefs and observations derived from our initial assumptions—that is, our first four non-commandments. It creates a contradictory worldview not governed by sense data or evidence. Even if we were to accept a particular God as a starting assumption, is it possible to live and function without assuming that our senses are the only way we perceive reality? Some people can—and do. But the rational mind cannot. With so many varieties of God, can you really be comfortable assuming that your own god is the right one? Some people can—and do. But the honest heart cannot.

Furthermore, as we've already seen, the God assumption isn't very useful unless we make several additional assumptions about what that God is like.

It comes down to this: if we acknowledge that a belief in God is a matter of faith and not evidence, then we also need to acknowledge that the attributes of God are also faith-based. In other words, every time we assume a God, we also have to make several additional assumptions about that God—that God is just, all-knowing, eternal, and so on.[14] Each of those assumptions carries with it more uncertainty, which you'll remember is exactly why we favor simplicity. That is, the fewer assumptions we have to make to explain reality, the more likely the assumptions we *do* have are valid. You might even call this another reason the God assumption is probably false: when you add that assumption, and all the other assumptions that have to come with it, the loss of simplicity takes our confidence down with it. In other words, every additional belief in God requires not just a little bit of faith but a whole lot of faith about a whole lot of different things *about* God.

But how do the framework of belief we have developed and our Ten Non-commandments deal with events or concepts that we can't perceive with our senses? For example, how can we respond to the question, *How did the universe begin?*

The system of belief we've developed sheds no light on this mystery. So is the system incomplete if it doesn't answer every question in the world? After all, religion does offer answers about how the world began—so perhaps that system has more merit?

The problem here lies with our system of language, logic, and grammar—what we've called "definitional truths." That system doesn't allow for something without a beginning or an existence without a creator. No system that uses our current tools of language and logic can ever resolve such a paradox. A belief in a God doesn't really answer the question—it just sends the question one step further back. *How did the universe begin?* becomes *How did God begin?* and so on. Like the description of the elderly lady's universe, it is turtles all the way down.

Instead of replacing one question with another and pretending we've answered anything, the most honest approach to questions beyond our comprehension is to state what we weren't allowed to say in the small white room: *I don't know.* That means that we admit the answer is simply beyond our current ability to conceive or even define appropriately with language.

What we are not saying is that science cannot in principle discover knowledge about the origin of the universe. Indeed, scientific discoveries such as the big bang theory, black holes, and dark matter are our best current attempts to find the answer. But even if we do figure out the origin of the universe, another question will be waiting in the wings: *What came before the origin?* Some things are just beyond our current abilities to think and express. But that doesn't mean we have to fall back on the God assumption.

Believers in God will no doubt have objections to this reasoning. Some of the most common of these objections are:

- The different gods are actually the same God, and we can set aside the petty differences between the various versions of God for a view of a common shared God.
- Since the lottery ticket is worth so much—a place in heaven—shouldn't you buy a ticket just in case you might win, no matter what the odds? This is known as Pascal's Wager.[15]
- There is corroborating, observable evidence for a belief in God in the form of ancient and modern miracles testified to in various holy books and by witnesses.
- A belief in God is necessary to give us hope; it makes the suffering in the world more tolerable and it motivates people to be moral.

Each of these objections has several flaws. But because they aren't relevant to the tasks at hand—creating Ten Non-commandments for the Twenty-first Century—we've addressed these objections in appendix A, "Common Religious Objections." Feel free to turn there at any time.

THE FIFTH NON-COMMANDMENT

Now that we've established that it's much more reasonable to assume God doesn't exist—the central claim of atheism—we can add this belief to the list of Ten Non-commandments, giving us:

I.   The world is real, and our desire to understand the world is the basis for belief.
II. We can perceive the world only through our human senses.
III. We use rational thought and language as tools for understanding the world.
IV. All truth is proportional to the evidence.
V.   *There is no God.*

6

PUTTING FACTUAL
BELIEFS TO THE TEST

It is hard enough to remember my opinions, without also remembering my reasons for them!

—Friedrich Nietzsche

We're now halfway home—five down and five to go—so it's a good time to look back at what we've built so far. We've used observations, inductive reasoning, the scientific method, and the idea of favoring simplicity to create five solid principles. We've also decided that it's best to reject belief in all things supernatural, including gods, and accept that we are each influenced by our subjective experiences, exposure to information, and our own intellect.

So far we've moved along with fairly simple examples like whether the sun will rise. Now let's broaden the scope, applying the non-commandments to more challenging problems to see how well our framework holds up. If we run into contradictions, or a principle springs a leak, we might have to circle back and reexamine our three core assumptions. Let's see what happens.

Since the belief system we've described relies so much on the subjective experiences of each individual, we'll need a volunteer to test-drive the framework and see what beliefs emerge. The lucky volunteer will need to share intimate, personal details about his or her life and innermost thoughts.

John has agreed to be the guinea pig for this section, and Lex the questioner. (We'll reverse the roles when we examine ethics and morals.)

John will offer his views to illustrate and test our emerging framework of belief, but remember, we are not claiming his views represent truth. They are just his best view of the truth given his own experiences and intellect.

But first a confession. So far we've been using probabilities in a way that works fine at low speeds—figuring out whether you left the lights on, for example, and assigning an equal chance to all principles. But it's not practical to assign probabilities to every variable in real life. There is no real-life Mr. Spock—the ultra-logical Star Trek character—to announce, "Captain, I estimate our chance of success to be no greater than 4.3639 percent."

That said, we still must determine how much confidence to have in a particular idea. We'll do this by deciding whether a source is trustworthy and how much personal experience we have in a given situation. Instead of using precise probabilities, let's divide our spectrum of belief into five broad categories:

1. I believe that is true.
2. I tend to agree with that opinion
3. I don't know.
4. I'm skeptical of that opinion.
5. That's nonsense.

The first and last categories are pretty straightforward. Either there is sufficient evidence to give you confidence to say, "Yes, I believe that," or there's enough doubt for you to reject it outright. But as nice as it would be for all of life to fall into these two strict categories, in practice we have to accept gray areas where answers are better stated as opinions rather than beliefs. (To be clear, even the strong convictions on either end are still opinions, but we treat them more as settled questions in everyday life. We can't be absolutely sure the stoplight that *looks* red actually *is* red, but we will go ahead and brake anyway.) If an assertion lands somewhere in the middle, and it's important enough ("Did I leave the car keys on the coffee table?"), then we look for additional evidence to drive our confidence up or down.

Even though "I don't know" technically covers everything in the middle, in real life we can't just leave it there unless the odds really are about fifty-fifty; otherwise, the belief just doesn't matter much. The realities of life often force us to take a stand even when we may not precisely *know* what to believe. For most of human history, "I don't know" has been a terrible conclusion to stand upon. A tendency to say, "I don't know if that rustle in the bushes is a lion," and to continue whistling down the path would eventually get the blissful agnostic removed from the gene pool.[1] Better for us to either assume the worst or increase our confidence one way or another.

Also, to answer, "I don't know" (such as to the question "Does God exist?"), is often taken to mean that such a belief is at least feasible or cannot be disproved. To avoid this misconception, we are more inclined to form an educated presumption of what to believe.

Speaking of which, it's time to begin that test drive. Using the five levels of how we classify our beliefs, let's see where someone who embraces our first five non-commandments falls on a few random topics.

Lex: John, do you believe that brushing your teeth every day will reduce your chance of tooth decay?

John: Yes. Not only do I believe it, but I've experienced the consequences of failing to brush my teeth properly when I had a cavity when I was young. That was more than enough to teach me that it's worthwhile to take a few extra minutes each day to care for my teeth. And I don't forget to floss, either.

Lex: That's one I need to work on myself—flossing more regularly. Let's move on to something without that kind of directly observable evidence. What is matter made out of?

John: Matter consists of atoms, and each atom is composed of a nucleus and a cloud of electrons. Even though I can't see the atoms themselves, I learned about them in chemistry in high school. I also see evidence of the effects of electrons, for example, such as the electricity powering my laptop and photos I've seen rendered by electron microscope imaging. Nuclear reactors are another good example of electrons, neutrons, and protons at work. The electron and nucleus is the simplest explanation for all of these things that I am aware of. I learned about basic atomic structure of atoms initially in science class and have also had conversations about this with knowledgeable people I trust. I regard their opinions as a form of testimony about the accuracy of this knowledge. But I can't directly perceive these elements of the atom, and I don't have a deep technical background in physics; so I'd categorize this belief as a strong opinion.

Lex: Okay, let's try to make things a bit more interesting. How about this: Do you believe aliens have visited Earth?

John: No, I don't believe that. The so-called evidence for this tends to be spotty enough to make me think that reported sightings and alleged alien encounters are probably either hoaxes or cases of mistaken perception. I'll go with the simpler explanation that some people have been deceived, are deluded, or are lying rather than the idea that multiple aliens have visited our planet but left no concrete evidence of having been here.

Lex: Fair enough—but what about the possibility that humans will make contact with intelligent life on another planet?

John: That's even more conjectural—you're asking whether we some-day will?

Lex: Yes, at some point in the future. What do you think?

John: This is a tough one, because there's so little to go on, but I guess I'd have to say no. I have no evidence to support such an opinion, so inductive reasoning isn't going to be much help. I have to use indirect evidence to work out the probability. Because the universe is so vast and the distance between stars is so great, even if there happened to be intelligent life-forms on another planet, the only way we could en-counter them is if they (or we) develop faster-than-light travel. This is something considered impossible by many physicists. They would also have to point themselves (or ourselves) in the exactly right direction for us to find each other. So I'd say I'm skeptical of meeting intelligent life from another planet, but I wouldn't say it's nonsense. I'll remain skepti-cal until better proof comes along.

Lex: Do you believe in ghosts?

John: Ghosts? No, I don't. I've never seen serious evidence for their existence, despite the subject getting plenty of attention from TV shows like "Ghost Hunters" and "Celebrity Ghost Hunters." You'd think that one of these shows would be able to muster up *some* reasonable evidence for ghosts if they existed, but all they manage are not-very-special ef-fects. Even worse than the lack of evidence is the lack of logic in the accounts we do get from people who claim to have seen them.

Consider a few common depictions of ghosts: there's the ghost clad only in a tattered bedsheet, the ghost dressed in Colonial attire, or the spooky Dickensian "Christmas Carol" ghost bound in heavy chains. Consider what each of these versions of ghosts is asking us to believe. Not only are we supposed to accept that human beings survive their bodily death and ascend to the spiritual plane, but their clothes and ac-cessories apparently cross over as well. Do clothes have a spiritual exis-tence? Are they damned to the human realm to resolve some unfinished business? Or are ghosts haunted by their clothes?

Lex: "Are ghosts haunted by their clothes?"—I'll bet that's the first time anyone has uttered that sentence! While we're on ghosts, do you believe in life after death?

John: No, I don't. Some people might say "I don't know" is a more appropriate answer since I've never experienced death. But I think we have enough information based on what I have encountered to make a reasonable conjecture. I've never encountered a mind without a brain. So if the brain dies, it's reasonable to assume the mind that lives in that brain dies with it. To believe in life after death, I'd have to believe in some supernatural concept like reincarnation or a soul. But while religions offer plenty of detail about the afterlife, they're awfully quiet on just how the soul survives death.[2]

People who believe in a soul or afterlife would have to explain not just how an immaterial soul could interact with a physical body, but also how this soul could be me and not just be a copy of part of me, at which point we're sailing in Theseus's Ship.[3] I'd need to believe that there's a nonphysical element in every person—and that's a much more complex solution than disbelieving in life after death. As you know, I think simplicity offers the best path to the truth. I'd certainly prefer to keep existing after I'm dead, but there is just no meaningful evidence for it. In fact, it's so improbable that it's irrelevant to the way I live my life.

The only way I could ever conceive of a form of "afterlife" would be through scientific developments that allow the brain of a person to keep functioning separated from its original body through a brain transplant or some brain-in-a-vat scenario. Or perhaps, if Ray Kurzweil's prediction comes true of the "singularity"—a time when computers will be able to replicate the human mind. So I'm a skeptic here. I think beliefs in the afterlife or reincarnation are more likely products of wishful thinking than accurate and honest assessments of reality.

Lex: Here's something more down-to-earth: Do you believe the stock market will go up tomorrow?

John: Gee, I hope so. But I have absolutely no idea about that. As far as I can tell, the movement of the stock market on any particular day is pretty much impossible to predict, especially for the layperson. Traders at firms like Goldman Sachs have more knowledge and experience than I do, as well as access to more information than I do, so they might make better guesses than I do. But they aren't infallible, and no one can predict the market perfectly all of the time.

We can see some clear patterns in John's personal beliefs. He has a strong belief in the scientific method and trusts evidence that comes from his personal experience or is corroborated by people he trusts. He doesn't believe in any supernatural phenomena—gods, ghosts, life after death—for the very simple reason that he hasn't had any experience with such phenomena and favors simplicity over accepting the supernatural into his view of reality.

What about questions such as, "Is euthanasia ethical?" or, "Is murder immoral?" These are also vitally important questions, and our framework and non-commandments still haven't provided us with any tools for answering such questions. But we'll get there shortly.

In this chapter, we haven't added any new beliefs to our Ten Non-commandments for the Twenty-first Century, but we have tested our initial core assumptions and the first five non-commandments. They seem to be working pretty well and holding up. To recap:

I.   The world is real, and our desire to understand the world is the basis for belief.
II.   We can perceive the world only through our human senses.
III. We use rational thought and language as tools for understanding the world.
IV.   All truth is proportional to the evidence.
V.   There is no God.

II

A FRAMEWORK FOR ETHICS

7

FROM BELIEFS TO BEHAVIOR

Happiness is a direction, not a place.

—Sydney J. Harris

The decisions we make every day are often more complex than just trying to figure out what is real. We also need to decide how we should behave. The transition from a worldview based on facts and data to a worldview about ethics and morals is not obvious. How can we link these seemingly disparate spheres of knowledge? How can we go from questions about existence (questions about what *is*) to questions about right and wrong (questions about what *ought* to be)?

Let's start by asking the question, *How should we behave?*

Can we use our framework for discerning what is real to shed light on what we ought to do? Perhaps if we rephrase the question to be more in line with a question about what is or is not, it will be easier to make some progress. Instead of asking how we should behave, let's ask, *What motivates our behavior?*

This is a question about reality, so it still falls within the framework of belief we've developed. This includes such tools as the senses to perceive the world around us and our intellect to decide what to believe based on these observations.

But what evidence can we gather to understand what motivates our behavior? The main source is the "observations" we can make about our thoughts and feelings when making decisions. In other words, we can use our own personal introspection as our guide.

Using introspection instead of direct observation is a little different from what we've done so far. Up until now we've talked about using our five senses to explore the external world. But when examining our own thoughts, we are not actually using any of those five senses. We are just aware of the thoughts in our minds.

These "observations" are still consistent with the framework of belief we've already developed. As part of that framework, as you may remember, we accepted the use of language and thought (the third non-commandment). This includes the ability of the mind to organize thoughts, find links between ideas, and draw conclusions. We also acknowledged that we have an ability to perceive thoughts.

A thought can be regarded as a real thing—it exists if you perceive it, and doesn't exist if you haven't yet consciously perceived it. To make an analogy to our other senses, perceiving your thoughts is like listening. Just as you can listen to music in the distance and reach a conclusion on the existence or nonexistence of that music, you can "listen" to the ponderings of your mind and reach a conclusion about whether or not a thought or desire exists.

Returning to the question of what motivates our behavior, we can rephrase it as, *What thoughts or desires exist in our minds when we are deciding how to act?*

Our first impulse when choosing how to behave is to gratify our own desires and inclinations. When we feel hungry, we try to relieve our hunger. When we feel lonely, we seek out the company of others. When the length of our hair grows irritating, we get haircuts. We have a natural inclination to satisfy our desires, which come in many forms. Some are clearly innate or biological, like the desire for food, warmth, and sex. Others can be more abstract, such as the desire for power, material wealth, social status, or intelligence. Are these desires independent motivators, or do they all have something in common?

Just as most beliefs about facts are based on other beliefs, most desires are based on other desires. Say you want to buy a new home. If we asked why you have this desire, you might reply that you want a home with more space and in a better school district. *Why do you desire a home with more space?* You want to start a family and need space for a kid's room, and you want to be in a neighborhood with good schools so your kids can get a good education. *Why do you desire a good education for your kids?* Because well-educated people tend to get better opportunities in life. *Why do you desire better opportunities for your kids?* This can go on for quite a while until we finally arrive at your set of fundamental source desires.

If we each reflect on our own personal desires and keep asking what the motivation is behind each layer of desire, it eventually becomes evident that all desires boil down to a single fundamental desire to seek happiness—a state of well-being and contentment—and avoid pain, whether physical or emotional. Happiness can arise both through physical pleasures, such as basking in the warmth of the sun, and through emotional ones, such as feeling loved. Receiving a gift can create feelings of happiness. Hearing bad news brings pain. Being praised can bring joy; being insulted can bring pain. So when we refer to happiness, we aren't speaking only about the good but also about avoiding the bad.

We can expand this notion of happiness even further to include both the short-term and the long-term perspectives. To capture this broader concept of happiness—which includes both physical and emotional pleasures and pains, as well as our estimate of all expected short-term and long-term happiness—let's use the term "life-happiness."

Life-happiness is an estimate of the total amount of happiness and pain you anticipate experiencing during your life. The balancing act between short-term and long-term happiness can be quite complicated because we often need to sacrifice some of that short-term happiness in exchange for greater happiness in the long term. For example, a child who gets an inoculation shot at her doctor's office might cry, but we know that the pain of the shot pales in comparison to the life-happiness she'll gain by avoiding contracting a preventable disease.

We can make an analogy between life-happiness and the financial concept of a company's market capitalization ("market cap"). Just as a company's value includes assets and liabilities, our concept of life-happiness factors in both the happiness and sadness in one's life. The fair market price of a stock at any point in time is supposed to reflect not just the shareholders' best estimate of the value of a company at that moment but also their estimate of its earnings and debts projected into the future.

In analyzing the prospects for a company, different weight can be placed on the value of current assets and earnings compared with expected future growth, depending on the type of company and where it is in its development. So the market cap of a young company often weights future projected earnings more heavily than those of mature enterprises. As market events unfold, or industry trends become clearer, the stock price of a company is adjusted accordingly.

The same is true for assessing life-happiness. We can guess at the sum total of happiness we'll experience over the course of our lives. New situations or realizations can affect our estimate of the expected happiness and pain we might experience in our lives. In our twenties, we don't generally value good health as much as we do if we reach our sixties. And at every stage, the tradeoff between short-term and long-term happiness varies, even within the same person, depending on state of mind, general outlook toward the future, and the type of experience in question.

Returning to the question posed earlier—*What motivates our behavior?*—we now have our answer. Our behavior is motivated by our desires, and these desires are in turn based on an urge to maximize our own life-happiness.

Simply put, all behavior is motivated by a yearning for happiness in life.[1]

Suppose a genie magically appeared and offered you a guarantee to experience the best life you were capable of living. Who wouldn't accept? While there are no genies (alas), we each attempt to grant ourselves the same wish by continually balancing and optimizing our short-term and long-term expected happiness.

Philosopher Jeremy Bentham said it best when he wrote:

> Nature has placed mankind under the governance of two sovereign masters, pain and pleasure. It is for them alone to point out what we ought to do, as well as to determine what we shall do. On the one hand the standard of right and wrong, on the other the chain of causes and effects, are fastened to their throne. They govern us in all we do, in all we say, in all we think.[2]

But how do we know what leads to our own happiness? We have to know what will make us happy if we're going to pursue it. It may seem that we just *know* we like cheesecake more than chocolate cake. But that knowledge, like most knowledge about what increases our happiness, isn't simply innate. Instead, it's most often gained from experience. A preference for cheesecake over chocolate cake usually follows years of eating both kinds, and a lot of others, and these "experiments" help us map out our own preferences.

By continually trying new things, we usually learn that our preferences change over time. Most kids don't like spicy food, and most adults don't like sugar-blasted cereal. Our internal "happiness meters" are calibrated and recalibrated through time and experience.

But that raises its own question: if we're projecting forward to maximize our life-happiness into the future, how do we factor in things we haven't experienced yet? We're not saying that in order to understand what will make us happy we need to experience *everything*. Even if it weren't impossible, such a strategy would be both undesirable and would waste lots of time. Instead, another form of real-life experience can be useful—reports from other, proven-reliable people.

Just as we weigh the testimony of others to form beliefs about facts, we can do the same thing to decide what we're likely to find pleasurable. By seeing what other people do and prefer, and asking them how they liked their experiences, we can learn about things we haven't tried or seen ourselves. You don't have to have an automobile accident to know that it's likely to reduce your happiness. You've heard from enough people who've experienced one. By the same token, when you were young, you probably knew your first kiss was likely to be something special because of the millions who had bravely gone before you.

Many of us have used this method of "polling" others' opinions when consulting the rating system for products on the online shopping website Amazon.com. These days, Amazon is more than just a bookseller. It's a big-data platform, aggregating the experiences of others to help you determine if you might like a particular product. Enough positive testimonials can increase your confidence in a product you haven't tried ("4.8 stars with 1,120 ratings? I'll take it!"). But if there are only two or three ratings, you might question whether those people are a good match for your own preferences. Meanwhile, Amazon is busily looking at your purchase patterns, comparing them to millions of other people—and presenting you with a short list of things you might also like to buy. When done well, this is extremely helpful, saving time, frustration, and money.

The social networking website Facebook.com provides another example of how we might learn from others about our own preferences and how we can gain confidence in which of our friends' tastes match our own:

- "Hmm, my friend Tom liked the page for a new tech gadget. I should check it out—Tom and I have the same appreciation for new technology."
- "Ellie likes a band called Rascal Flatts . . . but we almost never like the same music. I'm not going to pay much attention to her opinion on that."

In both cases, prior knowledge of past hits and misses by these "witnesses" allowed us to predict how well their suggestions, if followed, are likely to increase our own life-happiness.

Predicting what we'll like or dislike is complicated by conflicting choices. Let's go back to our scenario about buying a home. Should you purchase the one with the big outdoor patio or the one with the surround-sound TV room? What if you really like relaxing outdoors, but you also like watching movies? Which preference should carry more weight? You might also be juggling conflicts between short-term and long-term outcomes. Should you buy now, or will you experience greater long-term happiness by renting now, saving your money for a down payment, and buying a bigger house later? Experiences help us learn which paths usually lead to greater happiness, which in turn help us develop a general understanding about our own preferences.

Predicting how our actions today are likely to affect happiness down the road is a vital life skill. That's why, when our motivations conflict, we can spend a lot of time contemplating how events are likely to play out, how other people will probably respond, or how we're likely to feel in given situations.

When you're thinking about buying a home you also consider your desire not to be overburdened with a mortgage. You consider whether the home meets all of your requirements for size, features, and neighborhood. You estimate your income (as best you can) over the next thirty years and how stable your career is likely to be.

Finally, after all this thought and conjecture, you arrive at a decision: you'll buy the home. How did you finally decide? You weighed your various desires and how much happiness you expect each one to bring. You guessed how the various outcomes will affect you. And then, ultimately, you picked the one you thought would increase your life-happiness the most.

From this example, consider how much rational thought is involved in how we make decisions. As we can see, it may be used to influence, change, or police our motivations by changing estimates of our future happiness. But rational thought by itself doesn't compel action. It helps us figure out the likely outcomes and consequences of our desires, but a thought alone doesn't motivate action. It's the collision of thoughts and the desire for happiness that drives us to act.[3]

Buying a home is a huge life decision, so despite any pacing real estate agent, your careful consideration of the matter is entirely justified. But do we use the same process of analysis for smaller decisions? Not quite. Say you walk into a restaurant in your new neighborhood to celebrate becoming a homeowner. Sitting at the table, your decision is now merely between ordering the river trout or the rib-eye steak. Meanwhile, your decision, let's say, is complicated by your desire to keep your weight down and your cholesterol level low. The waiter's pencil is tapping his order pad impatiently.

You aren't likely to agonize over a decision about ordering dinner quite as much as buying a home, but the underlying process is the same. In the end, you will choose the meal that you think will maximize your life-happiness.

Perhaps you've done some research into the relationship between diet and cholesterol risk to help you determine what to eat. As a result, you no longer have to debate the overall strategy of what you consume every time you sit down for a meal. Rather, you now just follow the preferences and rules of thumb you've developed before. Every now and then you might revisit those preferences—after a visit to the doctor, perhaps, or after eating an amazingly tasty filet mignon—and adjust your preferences accordingly. But through all the twists and turns, you are always motivated by the desire to optimize your life-happiness.

Let's summarize:

1. We use experience, rational thought, and interactions with others to form expectations about what will make us happy.
2. Much of the rational thought involves speculating on the likely outcome of our actions.
3. Combine these expectations with the motive for happiness, and we're driven to action.

With these insights we now have a more comprehensive answer to the main question of what motivates our behavior:

Behavior is motivated by our beliefs about how best to increase our life-happiness, and these beliefs are based on our experiences in life.

But isn't the notion that we all try to maximize our life-happiness something impossible to prove? After all, we can't read each other's minds, so how can we ever *really* know what motivates someone else? If your life-happiness preferences are based on your own experiences and inclinations, and no one else can ever really get inside of your head, how can another person ever know for sure that you really are trying to increase your life-happiness?

We can't. But do we need to? The notion that all desires come from a fundamental desire for life-happiness doesn't come from watching what other people do—it comes from thinking about *our* own behavior and motivations and from asking other people what drives *their* own decision-making in this area. If we each analyze the thoughts and desires in our heads when we're choosing what to do, the motivation to aim for happiness is pretty clear.

We can also come to believe, through observations in life and through the findings of science, that most of the basic workings of one human being are the same as any other human being, including the mechanisms of the brain. The "happiness chemicals" serotonin and dopamine aren't reserved for a select group of people. Research has shown that these chemicals are an intrinsic aspect of moderating and controlling the human brain.[4] As a popular nerdy T-shirt puts it succinctly, "Serotonin and dopamine: technically, the only things you enjoy."

If we believe our own behavior is motivated by the pursuit of life-happiness and our observations of other people's behaviors confirm that they are doing the same, and if science validates the notion of happiness as a primary function of the brain, then we can reasonably say that most people are probably motivated by the pursuit of life-happiness.

Do we always maximize our own life-happiness? Of course not. Millions of people choose to smoke cigarettes. People get into debt gambling. There's a difference between trying to maximize our happiness and actually, successfully, doing it. We can be misled about what will give us the most happiness—by the addictive nicotine in cigarettes, for example, or by misunderstanding the odds of winning at the roulette wheel.

Sometimes we simply guess wrong about how events will unfold, or even how we'll feel in a given situation. Other times, we can be lazy and not take a moment to think things through. And, as we all know, we can also sometimes overestimate the likelihood of something happening or underestimate its impact on our emotions. It's pretty difficult to predict the future, especially when such predictions are over the extent of an entire lifetime.

This doesn't mean our motives aren't based on maximizing our life-happiness. It just shows that we are human beings—and sometimes we make decisions that turn out badly in the long run.

Where do emotions fit into our motivations? Many people think of emotions as something separate from the intellect. But in fact they are biologically linked. Emotions are, after all, a type of thought produced in the center region of the brain, mostly in the hippocampus and amygdala regions.[5]

Recent research in neuroscience has shown that these regions of our brain are also involved in our reasoning and memory formation.[6] That helps explain why we all (fortunately) have the ability to make quick decisions that seem instinctual—what we often call "gut feelings." If you see someone being beaten mercilessly, you don't have to sift through all the ramifications that have led you to oppose brutality before you feel anguish. You feel it immediately, seemingly unconsciously. And when something heavy comes flying at your head, you don't calculate the relative densities of the object and your skull or the likely impact of a long hospital stay on your life-happiness. You *duck*.

Some of these intuitions are innate or biological, like the fight-or-flight response to danger. But others emerge because of insights we gained from thoughts and experiences in the past. If you're a first-year surgical resident, you might have an emotional response of discomfort at first when asked to cut into a patient's flesh. And who could blame you? But after you've done it a few dozen times and become acclimated to performing surgical incisions, your reflexive emotional response will be modified. Eventually you'll feel little, if any, emotional discomfort when beginning surgery.

Another illustration of how experiences can influence our emotions is a phenomenon called "trauma triggers." If an individual experienced (or witnessed) a very traumatic event in the past, such as a rape or attempted murder, he or she might feel an intense emotional response in the future when encountering a trigger associated with the event. For instance, if a bell was ringing during the murder, from that point on the sound of a bell might trigger feelings of fear, even though the trigger itself isn't threatening in any way. Psychologists work with these victims to change their emotional responses by exposing them repeatedly to those same triggers in a safe and nonthreatening environment. Over time, the patient's emotions associated with the trigger are reshaped by new thoughts and experiences, and the patient is habituated out of the fear response.

While we may not be able to change our emotional responses quickly, these responses can and do change over time with experience and reflection. As they relate to our life-happiness preferences, emotions can be seen as the stored results of well-ingrained preferences. Our initial emotional response is the response that we've taught ourselves best represents our life-happiness preferences. The struggle we experience at times between our emotions and our mind's ability to provide contrary reasoning is a struggle to identify our true life-happiness preferences. Are they the ones we had yesterday (the ones still ingrained in our emotional response), or are they the ones we are going to have tomorrow (which will shape our future emotional responses)? In other words, our inner emotional struggles are simply mental struggles over how we see our future selves and what we want our future life-happiness preferences to be.

Some people are more introspective than others, and tend more often to reconcile their emotions with their thoughts. But the underlying mechanism for storing our preferences in the form of emotions occurs physiologically whether we think about them or not. In this sense, emotions aren't a separate motivating factor in our choices—they are embedded in the process itself. Emotions remind us of our current life-happiness preferences.

What about people who appear to openly shun the pursuit of happiness, such as ascetics—people who abstain from worldly pleasures to pursue religious and spiritual goals? What about Hindu sadhus who vow to stand only on one leg;[7] Jains who fast for extended periods;[8] Christian hermits who seclude themselves from all society;[9] and observant Jews who give up the myriad joys of a tasty cheeseburger? Suicides present yet another seemingly confusing counterexample. In these cases, a person is consciously choosing to forgo all future possible happiness.

While these extreme examples might appear to contradict our standard views of pursuing a life of happiness and avoiding pain, such behavior can still be seen as motivated by happiness preferences—albeit preferences that are foreign to most of us. For instance, ascetics derive more pleasure from their spiritual happiness and pride in their discipline than from the physical or emotional pains to which they subject themselves. As for people driven to suicide, many are experiencing such heartache and sadness that, at the moment they make the ultimate act, no possible future happiness seems capable of counteracting their pain. Indeed, suicide might be a rational choice for some people facing intense pain and suffering caused by an incurable illness.

Most of us tend to think about our life-happiness preferences within a standard healthy psychological model. But what about people who might suffer from addictions such as anorexia or alcoholism? Are they optimizing their life-happiness?

You might argue that people who have these psychological disorders are just bad at assessing how those behaviors will affect their lives. The anorexic might think that she will be more attractive if she is thinner but fails to grasp the long-term health impact starvation can cause. The alcoholic might fail to comprehend how his drunken behavior damages his relationships with others until his wife leaves him and takes the kids. Our ability to predict how our behaviors might affect our lives will always be flawed and imperfect. Once again, although we strive to optimize our life-happiness, we don't always succeed.

THE SIXTH NON-COMMANDMENT

The claim that we all attempt to maximize our life-happiness preferences might seem at first blush to be an overly selfish view. Nowhere yet have we discussed the role of morals in the decision-making process. Surely this has an impact on our motivations? Absolutely—our morals do have an impact on out motivations. That will be the topic of the next chapter.

For now, adding the notion of life-happiness to the list of Ten Non-commandments, we have:

I. The world is real, and our desire to understand the world is the basis for belief.

II. We can perceive the world only through our human senses.

III. We use rational thought and language as tools for understanding the world.

IV. All truth is proportional to the evidence.

V. There is no God.

VI. *We all strive to live a happy life. We pursue things that make us happy and avoid things that do not.*

8

HOW "OUGHT" ONE BEHAVE?

It would be very nice if there were a God who created the world and was a benevolent providence, and if there were a moral order in the universe and an after-life; but it is a very striking fact that all this is exactly as we are bound to wish it to be.

—Sigmund Freud

Up to this point we've only been talking about how we *do* behave. But we haven't yet answered the question of how we *should* behave.

The form of the question is particularly interesting. It assumes there *is* a "should," which implies some greater reason, purpose, or obligation—maybe even an authority—that dictates how we are supposed to behave.

To explore this notion of obligation further, let's consider the following two statements evoking obligation:

Statement 1: "I can't join you tonight because I have to finish my work."

Statement 2: "I feel obliged to visit my sick mother in the hospital tomorrow."

The language of these sentences implies that there's an unnamed motivation compelling the speaker to action. We could reveal the mystery motivator in statement 1 by adding that the speaker's supervisor has ordered him to finish his work. In statement 2, we might add that since his mother cared for him whenever he was sick as a child, the speaker feels obligated to care for her now. Intrinsic to any expression of "ought" is the notion of some external motivating factor dictating what needs to be done.

If we suppose for now that no such higher motivator exists, and also that our speaker has the ability to control his own actions, the above two statements can then be modified to read:

Statement 1: "I cannot join you tonight because I *choose* to finish my work."

Statement 2: "I *choose* to visit my sick mother in the hospital tomorrow."

The impact of this simple word-substitution on these two sentences is huge. It removes the idea of obligation from the actions. Instead, the actions are governed by individual choices and desires. To go one step further, these choices can then be stated in terms of preferences for happiness. Recasting our two statements in this manner yields:

Statement 1: "I cannot join you tonight because I choose to finish my work, *and pleasing my boss will probably provide me with greater long-term happiness than risking his anger for missing a deadline by spending the evening with you.*"

Statement 2: "I choose to visit my sick mother in the hospital tomorrow *because I know when I see the smile on her face when I arrive that her happiness will make me feel very happy.*"

These two examples show that it's possible to recast statements of obligation as choices about happiness. Two concepts are essential to do this. First is that we're all capable of making our own choices. Second is that nothing else forces us to act in a particular way other than our own thoughts, desires, and environment.

Let's address these one at a time.

Are we capable of making choices? Just as we can make observations about the world around us, we can make observations about the type of thoughts and desires that exist in our mind when taking actions. We're all intuitively aware of our ability to act as independent agents. We first gain awareness of our ability to control our own limbs as toddlers and to use our bodies toward our own ends. We learn to reach for a bottle in order to eat or to bang on the kitchen table to get some attention. As our development continues, we learn about delayed gratification and how to exhibit self-restraint. By our teens, we develop the ability to align our actions with our intentions and gain a sense of our ability to act as independent agents.

A famous study called the Stanford marshmallow experiment tested the idea of "delayed gratification" in young children. Conducted in the

1960s, the study tested preschoolers to see if they could delay gratification.[1] Each child would sit alone in a room with a marshmallow, Oreo, or pretzel stick (whatever the child preferred) for fifteen minutes. The child was told that, if he or she hadn't eaten the treat after that interval, he or she got a second treat. As it turned out, just one-third of the six-hundred participants waited long enough to get a second treat. Would the outcome have been the same if the study were conducted on adults? Probably not. We are increasingly able to delay gratification as we age,[2] and by the time we reach adulthood, skills such as self-restraint and self-control are well entrenched.

Of course, some physiological needs are impossible to completely suppress. We all need to eventually breathe, urinate, or sleep. While we might be able to suppress or delay these impulses temporarily, ultimately they are beyond our realm of self-control. But when we talk about the ability to make choices, we're talking about voluntary behavioral choices, not the life-giving functions of bodily organs.

We've each seen how our own choices affect the outcomes of events around us. What clothes do we choose to put on each day? What words do we choose to say? How do we choose to kiss a lover? Choices confront us throughout each day, and we can observe our ability to make choices independently. Through these personal observations and through introspection, we can conclude that we do indeed have the ability to choose how to behave.

There are limits to our ability to choose, of course. Genetic makeup and environmental factors provide constraints. We can't choose to fly. We can't choose to be a foot taller. A person who only knows English can't instantly choose to speak Spanish. Constraints around our abilities, intellect, life circumstances, and financial resources abound and limit our choices, and some people are more limited by these circumstances than others. Our ability to choose how we act just means that whenever we face a choice of actions that we *can* take, we have the ability to choose among them. The concepts of "preferences," "desires," and "wants" would have no meaning if we lacked the ability to choose how we act.

Some people contend that choice is merely an illusion and that all of our actions are dictated not by choice but by the laws of physics. This argument goes as follows: Our bodies are composed of matter—atoms, elements, chemicals, cells. Our bodies follow the laws of physics, so our future actions aren't chosen by "us" but by our biochemical state.

The apparent conflict here is caused by a mismatch of reference frames. The first reference frame is at the atomic level, which looks at the world at the scale of atoms and particles. The second is at the psychological level, which looks at our minds as a collection of thoughts and memories. Both of these viewpoints are valid, but both have limitations to their domains of knowledge. They both have scopes of relevance, applicability, and terminology.

The atomic reference frame is valuable when designing semiconductors or nanotubes, but at larger scales it doesn't provide much useful information. The complexity grows too vast as the number of atomic interactions increases and the predictive power in a practical sense is reduced to zero.

But just for fun, imagine we could[3] describe a basketball game in terms of the motions of every one of the 10^{30} atoms colliding during the game.[4] You could even say the outcome of the game could be predetermined if we had perfect information about the state of all those atoms before the game began. But such a description wouldn't be very useful in explaining concepts such as "dunk," "pick and roll," and "three-pointer." These terms have no meaning in the reference frame of atoms colliding, but they have great relevance to understanding and enjoying the game of basketball.

Another example: if we gave you a choice between spending two hours reading the machine code for the videogame *Call of Duty* or two hours playing the game, which would you choose? Even though the machine code determines and describes what's happening on the screen, we know that there's an enormous difference between the experience and information presented when playing the game and the experience and information presented when studying its code.

That's why human beings have developed other reference frames for the study of these larger macro systems. Biologists study muscle behavior at the cellular level; oceanographers study sea currents at the oceanic level; and psychologists study behavior at the level of thoughts and memories. As theoretical physicist Sean Carroll has argued, while our mind's inner workings are no doubt tied to physical atomic interactions, those interactions do not discredit the psychological reference frame.[5] Rather, these two reference frames are simultaneously compatible. They just require us to look at the way the mind works with two different perspectives and terminology. It's at the psychological level, not the atomic level, that the notion of choice has descriptive power and meaning. And it's there, at the level of human psychology, that we're all aware of our ability to act as independent agents, to align our actions with our intentions, and to make decisions and choices.

That takes care of the first concept needed to recast statements of obligation into statements of preference and choice. Now let's consider the second: that nothing forces us to act in a particular way other than our own thoughts, desires, and environment.

It seems reasonable to think that if any such external motivating force were to exist, we might be forced to choose to obey the external motivator instead of acting independently and making an uncoerced choice.

What do we mean by an "external motivator?" If choice and preference are internal motivators, then an external motivator would be something separate from ourselves and our desires that drives us to choose certain actions. If a waiter held a gun to your head while you were dithering between the steak and trout and announced, "Order the trout or I'll shoot you!" that threat would be an external motivator (and probably a compelling one) for your decision.

A less extreme example can be found in the rule of law in our societies. The threat of punishment imposed by the legal system, such as jail time or a fine, regularly serves as an external motivator to influence our choices.

But when it comes to choosing how we behave, the external motivator most associated with ethical choices is morality. It's very common for people to express the reasons for their actions as following a moral code. In evaluating this form of external motivator, we can ask the simple question, *Does an objective moral truth exist?*

If an objective moral truth existed, it would likely be the prime motivator for our behavioral choices. Since this is a question about the existence or nonexistence of an entity, we can use the framework of belief we have developed (the first five non-commandments) to get the answer. This gives us a way to link the world of facts and observations with the world of behavior and ethics.

What does "objective moral truth" mean? An objective moral truth is a morality that exists independently of the way any person perceives it. It means that for any moral dilemma a person encounters, there's a predefined, precisely correct path of action, a "right answer."

Just as a belief in an objective reality implies that truth exists, so the notion of an objective morality implies that moral truths exist.[6] If we deny the existence of an objective morality, we are affirming the contrary—a subjective morality. Such a morality would not be a definitive, universal set of rules. Instead, it would exist only as it is interpreted or viewed by the people who rely on it, so it would naturally exist in many different forms.

At this point we can draw a parallel between the three core assumptions we made earlier about the nature of existence and the starting points we might need for a meaningful system of objective moral truth. Remember, to make progress on the question of what we should believe, we laid out three core assumptions that also established three central concepts: the acknowledgment of existence, a method for perceiving that existence, and tools for describing and thinking about that existence.

To make similar progress in the field of objective morality, we first need to determine whether an objective morality actually exists, then determine which ethical senses we are endowed with to perceive the moral truth, and finally determine what tools we can use to evaluate and think about morality.

The same tools of intellect, language, logic, and thought (what we called "definitional truths") still work for ethics, so we don't need anything new here. But to build a system of objective morality, we also need two new beliefs:

1. That objective moral truth exists.
2. That there is an ethical sensing faculty that allows us to perceive and evaluate the moral truth.[7]

Without these two beliefs, the parallel to the belief system we constructed for objective reality would fall short and the effort to generate a coherent system of universal objective ethics would seem insurmountable.

The faculty we use for sensing what is moral and what is not is that of our mind and intellect. Included with the intellect are the faculties of "emotion," or the "heart," as discussed earlier. These terms are merely a description for specific aspects of our mind's abilities. Emotions can be thought of as an impulse response that reflects deeply ingrained preferences acquired over time. And that makes our minds, which include both thoughts and emotions, our sensing faculty for perceiving ethics.

That said, there are differences. People perceive the world around them in very similar ways through their five senses, but we differ dramatically in the way our intellects perceive objective moral truth. In particular, our intellect seems to need much more interpretation and processing to reach a moral conclusion. By comparison, our senses are more mechanical in nature—they just perceive what is before them. For example, sight can be understood as light waves focused on the retina, stimulating impulses in rod and cone cells that transmit electrical signals to the brain, which interprets them as vision. Little subjective interpretation is necessary to perceive light. In this instance, there is a physical interaction that occurs between an external entity and our sense organs—photons interacting with nerve receptors. Similarly, the perception of sound is caused by the physical interaction between an external entity and our sense organs. External pressure waves traveling through the air into our ear canals cause the thin membranes of our eardrums to vibrate and allow us to recognize sound.

But no such interaction exists for moral sensing. We can reduce moral feelings to the mechanism of chemical concentrations in the brain, but the repeatable interaction, or communication, between some external moral entity and any internal moral "organ" is simply not evident. Rather, the interpretive ability of our mind in sensing morality is one that depends on the experiences we've had, not to mention our personality and outlook. So if we are forced to decide whether our ethical senses are perceiving an objective morality truth, or are forming a subjective morality, it surely seems the latter.

This discussion might seem silly. How can we possibly think of morality in the same way we think of physical objects? That's exactly our point— *we can't.* Morality cannot be thought of in the same absolute, unchanging way we think of physical things because there is an objective reality, but there is no objective moral truth.

What about moral principles that have been presented throughout history as objective moral truths?

There are five main categories of these allegedly objective moral codes: God-created moral codes, leader-created moral codes, consensus moral codes, human-designed moral codes, and duty. Let's look at each of them in turn.

GOD-CREATED MORAL CODES

God-created morality holds that all moral rules exist only by God's command. To follow his commands is to be moral.

Moral philosophers call this divine command theory.[8] Many religions set down in an absolute way how a person is supposed to behave—that is, which behaviors are moral and which are immoral. The Ten Commandments are an example of God-created morality and are by no means the only ones. The twelfth-century Talmudic scholar Maimonides counted the various laws, behaviors, and beliefs (*mitzvot*) that God prescribed in the five books of the Old Testament. The final count was 613 laws to be followed by observant Jews.[9]

A few examples from his list include to worship God (no. 6); for women not to wear men's clothing (no. 71); not to sleep with a woman before marriage (no. 123); a rapist should marry his victim if she is unwed (no. 132); not to have homosexual relations (no. 157); not to marry non-Jews (no. 163); not to eat shellfish (no. 178); not to eat dairy and meat together (no. 196); not to wear clothing made of wool and linen woven together (no. 238); to give to charity (no. 250); not to stand idly by if someone's life is in danger (no. 489); to pay wages on time (no. 519).

God-created morality isn't just a collection of the opinions of mere men, or of collective society, but the will of a supreme supernatural being. Our earlier conclusion that God doesn't exist presents an existential challenge to God-created morality. Without a God to attach it to, such a moral code loses any sanctity, as well as any claims to objectivity or truth. However, even if a God existed, we'd still run into that problem of having no way of knowing which of the gods is the correct one, meaning that there would be no way to tell which set of "godly" laws to follow.

LEADER-CREATED MORAL CODES

If we can't turn to the gods for moral guidance, what about human leaders? An example of a moral standard developed by a human leader is the Code of Hammurabi. Created in 1772 BCE by the ancient Babylonian king Hammurabi, this code provided basic moral rules for Babylonian society. An almost complete copy of the code survives on a stone tablet held at the Louvre.[10] The code consists of 282 laws. A few examples: if anyone is committing a robbery and is caught, then he shall be put to death (no. 22); if a son strike his father, his hands shall be hewn off (no. 195); if a man put out the eye of another man, his eye shall be put out (no. 196).[11] Not the most enlightened moral code by modern standards.

Can ruler-created moral codes qualify as objective moral codes? No. They can be dismissed as merely reflective of the views of the leaders of those societies who imposed them onto their subjects by force. We don't follow the Code of Hammurabi in the modern era because our own ethical concepts have evolved past those of the ancient world—a time in which (among other things) women were often considered the property of their husbands. We aren't particularly concerned with, or motivated by, what Hammurabi thought almost four thousand years ago, nor should we be.

CONSENSUS MORAL CODES

If the leaders of societies can't provide an objective moral code, then can objective moral codes arise from the moral consensus that has evolved over time? The moral zeitgeist is the moral spirit in a particular place and time—the consensus opinion.[12] Can the moral zeitgeist be considered an objective moral truth? If we get a high degree of agreement among people as to what is moral or what is not, could that indicate that we have found an absolute moral truth? If nearly everyone is against murder, for example, could that mean that "murder is immoral" is an objective moral truth?

Once again, let's take an analytical approach. If we had the ability to poll every person in a community on a particular moral question, and then analyze the responses, we could determine the most frequent responses. Sometimes we might even find that nearly everyone agrees on an issue; other times we might find that there is considerable debate. Theoretically, at any given point in time, there exists a precise answer as to what the most popular response to any given moral question would be. As long as we could record responses and count how many of each response we received, we would arrive at a populist moral standard, occasionally with nearly unanimous consent.

Instead of taking a poll to determine the exact moral responses of people, we might instead infer what the typical response would be through discussions with other people who make up a sample of the community. If we were to do this for all types of moral thoughts, we might develop an awareness of the typical moral inclination of the people around us and, in the process, determine the moral zeitgeist. Just as we, as individuals, are capable of forming impressions of what the most popular fashions and hairstyles are, we're also capable of forming impressions about the popular moral inclinations of our society.

By pulling together all of these subjective preferences, we might regard the current moral zeitgeist as approximating an objective moral standard. But there's a big difference between a standard based on popularity and one based on a truly objective moral code. In the end, the moral zeitgeist is just a collection of many *subjective* thoughts. It still lacks a form of moral truth that is independent of any one individual's ability to influence it.

Even if we could reach 100 percent agreement on a given moral issue—a very unlikely thing—it would still only mean that we have a consensus of subjective preferences, not a notion of objective moral truth. There was a near-unanimous consensus in many parts of the antebellum South that blacks and whites shouldn't intermarry and have children together, but few Southerners today would say that made it an objective moral truth. There is no level of consensus that could ever justify regarding our subjective preferences as objective moral truths.

To understand why, imagine if we wanted to create the objectively perfect cookie. You might think that a smart way to approach this problem would be by polling a large sample of people and having them test a variety of different cookie recipes under various conditions. But the reality is that we'd immediately run into problems. Some people like the Girl Scouts' Thin Mint cookies, some like chocolate chip cookies, and some people, for reasons unclear, prefer oatmeal raisin. Some like their cookies crispy, and some like them soft.

If we try to make a cookie that appeals to each person's ideal, we'd end up either with an incoherent mess of ingredients in an attempt to please everyone or a bland consensus cookie in an attempt to offend no one. There is no "best possible cookie," just as there is no "best possible poem," "best possible painting," or "best possible running playlist." As the old aphorism says, beauty is in the eye of the beholder, and there's no accounting for taste. However you put it, preferences are subjective; different people have different preferences, and they are often incompatible.

Even if we put aside for a moment the blunt reality that it's impossible to reach a complete consensus "best possible cookie," it would still be *entirely irrelevant* to the question of whether that recipe was an objectively perfect cookie. Instead, all we would have created is the current best cookie consensus. Our history is littered with consensus moral beliefs that were once wildly popular but seem utterly wrongheaded, even barbaric, to us in the rearview mirror of history. Women as chattel, human sacrifice, infanticide—the zeitgeist changes significantly over time.[13] As Steven Pinker argues persuasively in *The Better Angels of Our Nature: Why Violence Has Declined*, the consensus has evolved to be more sensitive to the moral concerns of more people over time.[14] This constant evolution is a great benefit as it recognizes that changes in human circumstances also require changes in moral perspective. But because consensus opinions change as the needs and desires of human beings change, this constant evolution also shows that consensus can't possibly serve as a universal objective moral truth.

HUMAN-DESIGNED MORAL CODES

If we can't create an objective moral code by averaging the moral preferences of individuals in a society, maybe we can design a universally binding code of ethics. As you can imagine, it has been tried many times. A few examples of human-designed moral codes include Jeremy Bentham's utilitarianism, Immanuel Kant's categorical imperative, and John Rawls's "veil of ignorance."

Utilitarianism is the idea that moral decisions should be made based on the principle of utility, providing the greatest happiness for the greatest number of people.[15] The system suggests that when you consider a moral conundrum, you should look at the consequences of choice A, B, C, and so on, and choose the one that produces the best consequences for the greatest number of people.

Kant's categorical imperative suggests that we should only act in a way that we think should be allowed for everyone in the same situation.[16] If you are considering becoming a thief, you should ask what the world would be like if theft were practiced by everyone. And since you wouldn't want people stealing from you, the categorical imperative leads you to conclude that stealing is immoral.

Rawls's "veil of ignorance" says we ought to make moral decisions from a blind perspective regarding our own status, skills, mental and physical capacity, and position in society.[17] If you were born with high natural intelligence and low athletic ability, you'll likely want to live in a society that rewards people of high intelligence, and you'll be indifferent whether athletes are rewarded for their skills. But that isn't fair to people born with low intelligence and high athletic ability. The only way to create fair circumstances, Rawls argues, is for us to ignore everything about us that positions us relative to others and then make ethical decisions blind to our own talents, skills, and capacities.

Do Bentham's, Kant's, and Rawls's philosophies meet the requirements of being absolute moral standards? Certainly they are universal in the sense that they apply to all people. But that isn't enough to elevate any of them to the one true moral code. Claiming to be universal doesn't make any of them automatically or exclusively valid.

As you may guess, each of these thinkers asserts that his moral code is universally binding, meaning everybody has to obey it whether they want to or not. One could similarly dream up many wicked moral codes and assert that they are universally applicable, too. How would we decide which moral code to pick? Kant, Rawls, and Bentham each considered their own axioms to be the ultimate source of moral goodness. It's unclear what a Kantian, Utilitarianist, or Rawlsian could say to each other to convince the others to abandon their asserted objective moral codes.

Imperatives demand a reason. When we hear a command, if we don't already understand the reason, we ask, "Why?" To simply reply, "Because I said so"—known as the appeal to authority—is technically a reason, but a pretty weak one. Because we don't generally act without reasons, a command that fails to provide or at least imply a reason fails to motivate us to act. You might also recognize a parallel to the "folly of the lottery ticket" here. Choosing one exclusive moral code out of so many potential choices[18] is as dicey a proposition as choosing one god out of thousands.

To meet the criteria of being an objective *truth*, these man-made moral codes would need to be objectively justified or to exist as an independent standard separate from any individual's ability to form them.

It should be added that the ideas captured by these moral theories are still meaningful and may very well play a role in how we make moral assessments. Concepts such as applying behaviors universally to everyone or examining ethical dilemmas from an unbiased position are powerful tools for examining ethics. But that doesn't mean that such standards imply the existence of an objective moral truth, much less that any of these moral codes is holding the winning ticket to the moral lottery.

DUTY AS MORAL CODE

Finally, another commonly cited manmade motivator is duty.[19] Do we really visit our mothers because their company makes us happy or because duty compels us to? You might say it depends on the mother.

But what is duty, really? The textbook definition is, "What one performs in fulfillment of the dictates of conscience, piety, right, or law."[20] In other words, duty is the name we give to nonphysical notions that compel us to act in a particular way.

When we say, "Duty requires us to act a certain way," we're really saying, "I've made a commitment to act that way, or my preexisting commitments require me to act that way." As a result, while duties might seem to be external motivators, they are not. Duties are simply a person's commitments. A person will only feel a duty to do things that relate to commitments he or she has made. Consider a daughter who loves her father dearly. She feels that the father-daughter bond creates a duty for daughters to visit their fathers. But if the daughter didn't love her father (maybe because he was abusive), she is less likely to feel this duty because she doesn't have a commitment to respect her father.

So duty isn't really an external motivator—it's an internal motivator, a specific type of life-happiness preference. Duty expresses a preference some of us have for honoring our commitments and regulating our own behavior when it comes to actions that, while they may lead to diminished short-term happiness, could lead to more significant long-term life-happiness.

This doesn't mean duty is an unimportant concept. A husband who remains faithful to his wife may claim this to be an act of duty, but it may also be his preference to avoid the potential consequences of hurting someone dear to him, being shunned by his family or friends, or feeling guilty about his behavior. The soldier who says she fights for her country out of duty may also be motivated by the life-happiness she expects to gain in the form of self-esteem, self-respect, and the praise she receives from others for her choice. Duty may well play a strong role in certain aspects of our decision-making process. Indeed, duties remind us of our commitments we've made to others in the past and help us choose our future commitments. The point at hand, though, is that duty is not a separate, independent force or an objective moral truth but part of the makeup of our choice preferences.

In summary then, neither God-created moral codes, leader-created moral codes, consensus moral codes, human-designed moral codes, nor duty satisfy the requirements for an objective moral truth.

Having shown that we possess the ability to choose how we act, and having found no objective moral truth, the question, "How ought we behave?" now seems semantically incorrect. It falsely assumes that there is some external motivator dictating how we should behave. Instead, we can answer the question as follows:

There's no one way we "ought to behave." We choose to behave in the way that we think optimizes our life-happiness.

Without an implied external motivator, our behavior is dictated by the pursuit of our own life-happiness and by our choices, rather than by any supposed external moral obligation.

Of course, our life-happiness may very well be influenced by things like duty, popular opinion, ethical theories, culture, and religion. But even though we might choose to incorporate these influences into our subjective decisions, that doesn't make them objective moral standards. Rather, they are factors we may choose (or not choose) to incorporate into our ethical decision-making processes, based on our own subjective desires.

THE SEVENTH NON-COMMANDMENT

This chapter focused less on creating a new belief than on displacing a false one about obligation to an objective moral truth. As a result, we can now add the rejection of an objective moral truth to our list of non-commandments. But this non-commandment is not yet complete. We still have to explore where our morals *do* come from. In the next chapter we will explore what moral beliefs arise from a worldview based on choice and preference.

To recap the list of Ten Non-commandments, so far:

I.   The world is real, and our desire to understand the world is the basis for belief.

II.   We can perceive the world only through our human senses.

III. We use rational thought and language as tools for understanding the world.

IV.   All truth is proportional to the evidence.

V.   There is no God.

VI.   We all strive to live a happy life. We pursue things that make us happy and avoid things that do not.

VII. *There is no universal moral truth.*

More to come . . .

9

MORAL HAPPINESS

Human happiness and moral duty are inseparably connected.

—George Washington

Having failed to find even one objective basis for moral truth, we are left to conclude that morality is *subjective.*

That simple sentence is enough to give many people an anxiety attack. The belief that we *need* absolute objective morality runs deep and wide in most of us. As the psychologist William James put it, "We are all absolutists by instinct, and only by reflection can we achieve empiricist moderation."[1]

We're here to bring some of that empiricist moderation. But we do so humbly, because once upon a time we both believed in objective morality. John was a Kantian during college, and Lex as a teenager was a believer in the "objective moral duty" view of morality.

While reading some of the coming discussions, the idea of absolute moral truth might occasionally surface in your thoughts as the question, "How ought I behave?" But remember that we just spent a chapter rejecting the whole idea of "ought," or that there is an objectively correct way to behave. We'll revisit this point, since it's important to deal fully with the abandonment of an objective moral truth if we're going to keep moving forward.

Here's another sentence that might surface in some form in your mind: "A system of morality should tell you how to behave in any given situation." The hidden assumption here is that there's one absolute or correct way to behave in every situation. To believe in a subjective morality, on the other hand, is to recognize that a system of morality doesn't tell us how we ought to behave; it guides us in understanding our own thought processes and then lets each of us *choose* how to act.

91

But that leads to one of the most common concerns in any discussion of this kind: "If everything is subjective, then anything goes! All versions of morality are equally valid."

Frankly, this fear of complete moral relativism is misplaced. Even without an absolute moral truth, we can still have a meaningful conversation about right and wrong actions. It's true that claims about right and wrong can't be stated as certainties, but they can be stated as strong (and even enforceable) preferences. As a result, we can still debate ethical values by relating the preferences of the individual to the moral consensus preferences of society—that is, balancing what you want against what's best for everyone.

To explore the concept of subjective morality further and understand what it means, let's posit an individual named Pete. Pete will share with us intimate details about his upbringing and his personal experiences. First we'll look at how Pete might have formed his subjective moral outlook. Then we'll look at what motivates Pete to act morally. Finally, in the next chapter, we'll look at how Pete's morals fit in the context of a larger society and how societal influences affect his moral outlook.

As a child, Pete's upbringing and exposure to life were largely regulated by his parents. They decided if he could drink soda or coffee—and so played a key role in nurturing the types of pleasures he could cultivate at a young age. Their influence was even more profound at times when they made an effort to reward or punish certain behaviors. Pete was encouraged to share toys with his siblings and reprimanded when he did not. While his parents couldn't directly change Pete's innate inclinations, they were certainly able to cultivate or nurture certain behaviors they favored through access, rewards, and punishments—sometimes referred to as "parenting." So Pete's pleasure preferences were strongly influenced by his upbringing and life experiences as a child.[2]

As a young adult, Pete came to realize that he was free to make his own decisions. With this realization came the awareness that his parents' reprimands or encouragements no longer had the same controlling effect on his behavior that they once did. At this point, Pete began to ask himself, "Do I really enjoy doing this or that, or have I been behaving in a particular way just to please my parents?" In other words, does Pete really enjoy cheesecake, or does he enjoy it simply because he was told by his parents to eat it at his grandmother's house every Sunday? The answer is unclear, since Pete's current love of cheesecake is a product of both his own inclinations and the reality that he has many pleasurable memories of eating cheesecake at his grandma's. Pete's pleasure preferences as related to cheesecake are a combination of many influences and experiences. Although the exact source of his pleasure is imprecise, the question he faces today is quite clear: Does he really like cheesecake?

The answer to him is obvious—he does. His current set of pleasure preferences is now determined through his own personal choices, even if those choices originate from a period in his life when he didn't have the ability to choose freely.

There's a practical element to life that doesn't allow us to sit and contemplate the full consequences of every action we take. Instead, we tend to form rules of thumb as shortcuts to decision-making.

Pete may realize that his enjoyment of cheesecake falls under a much broader preference for sweet foods. So when he has a choice between two foods he's never tried before, Pete can use this guide to influence his choices. Extending this idea, Pete may develop a larger set of general guiding principles for his culinary choices, such as a preference for larger meals or for eating with others. We may refer to this set of general guides that Pete develops as his culinary preferences.

This example is a glimpse into how we form all of our behavioral preferences. The mechanism that creates Pete's food preferences is the same process that creates his broader preferences, including his moral preferences. His preferences are a combination of his personal tastes, experiences, and influences.

Viewed in this light, our system of ethics is just a collection of guiding principles and rules that we've collected over the years that encompass our preferences relating to a particular kind of behavior: interactions with other people.

Such a perspective makes some people anxious. They worry that if personal preferences and happiness are our only motivation, we would all become hedonists who selfishly pursue nothing but our carnal desires. That's overly simplistic.

First of all, the concept of life-happiness means that we are striving for an optimal balance between short- and long-term happiness. Most of us would agree that pursuing only one's carnal desires, while pleasurable in the moment, wouldn't lead to long-term happiness over the course of a lifetime. Second, there are other mechanisms within a system of pursuing happiness that can and do lead to "typical" moral behavior. Enlightened self-interest is one; identification with others is another.[3]

Enlightened self-interest is the idea that prioritizing your own concerns can lead you to behave in a way that is moral or beneficial for society.[4] A simple example of this is cooperation. Cooperation is often cited as a basic form of moral behavior since it requires treating other people with respect and consideration. Cooperative action can be a way for someone to maximize his or her own self-interest. For example, if Pete has a close friend who asks for his help moving into his new apartment, Pete may decide to help because his friend will be more likely to return that help someday. That's enlightened self-interest.

A formal development of this mechanism is found in the study of "game theory." Game theory demonstrates that in certain situations, individuals pursuing self-interest in a group environment will choose to cooperate with others to get the best outcome for themselves. It turns out that individuals often fare better in a community of interdependent people than in one in which it's every man for himself.

The study of game theory often involves simplified social experiments in which people play various "games" in a lab setting. The behavior of the subjects is monitored while they interact with other people (or a computer program) in situations with predefined rules. A typical example is the ultimatum game. Pete will interact with another player, Rachel, for one hundred interactions. The game works by alternately granting Pete and Rachel ten dollars and having each offer some amount of the money to the other person. The one on the receiving end can either accept that offer or ask the proctor to take back the entire ten dollars. With rules defined in this way, subjects tend to settle into the same type of behavior—they share the money. Why? Let's say Pete keeps making meager offers such as giving just one or two measly bucks to Rachel. Instead of taking the dollar, Rachel may decide to reprimand Pete by having the proctor take back the full ten dollars so they both end up with nothing. Pretty soon, Pete is going to realize that he needs to increase his offers to Rachel if he wants to see any money himself—something much more fair, like five dollars. Rachel responds by rewarding the "fair play" with the same behavior when it's her turn. And so the two players settle on a strategy in which they both maximize their own profits by sharing the money every time. The sooner the players learn to cooperate, the greater their profits will be.

It's easy to see the implications for the real world. People who develop a reputation for cooperating fairly are more likely to receive additional offers to cooperate, while those who prove themselves poor collaborators will find others hesitant to cooperate with them.

Game theorists don't just rely on repeating experiments with human subjects. They also run large computer simulations with set rules and interactions to determine the optimum strategies for certain interactions. Several basic models have emerged from this field of study. In a game where people have continued interactions, a person can typically maximize his or her profits (or happiness) by cooperating with others and by punishing those who do not cooperate. In other words, cooperation often leads to greater personal happiness. Punishing others who don't cooperate serves to preserve a world of cooperation and remind people that it's in their best interests to cooperate.[5]

While game theory has formalized our understanding of human interactions, experience has taught us that such results are to be expected. Examples where cooperation can lead to a greater state of happiness for an individual in a group are common and deeply rooted in our behavior. Kids learn early on that two of them may be able to carry the chair to the high kitchen cabinet to pull off a cookie heist, even if they then have to share the loot. People in the world of business and politics frequently trade favors.

This desire for cooperation can be used to explain many types of moral behavior in society. We've developed certain skill sets that promote these kinds of interactions, such as the ability to keep mental logs about the way different people have treated us in the past. As a society, we regularly promote the spread of this type of information—whether a particular individual tends to interact fairly with others—by referring to people's reputations.[6]

While enlightened self-interest and game theory help explain why people who seek happiness will act in "moral" ways, it's not the full story. While in certain situations the pursuit of happiness may lead to cooperation, in other situations, noncooperative behavior is advantageous—especially when the individuals in a group are not likely to encounter each other again. Game theory is heavily dependent on the starting conditions of the game and the use of repeated interactions. In real life, people's power or wealth can be heavily asymmetric. With a world population of more than seven billion, single and anonymous interactions are common. So how do we explain moral behavior that's not grounded in game-theory-type repetitions?

For that, we turn to the second mechanism for encouraging moral behavior: *identification with others.*

The pursuit of happiness isn't the same as *complete* self-interest with no concern for what others need and want. It's also quite common to find happiness in observing the happiness of others.[7] Just as we feel happiness and pain, we understand that other people prefer happiness just as much as we do. Out of empathy—the ability to feel what others are feeling—we derive happiness from observing the happiness of others, even if their happiness doesn't directly affect our own lives. And the inverse—feeling sadness or heartache from seeing another person or animal in pain—is often even stronger.

Neuroscientists have observed this phenomenon in studies involving fMRI brain scans (a tool that provides a real-time visualization of brain activity). When we see someone else smile, cry, or bang a shin on a coffee table, the same neural pathways light up in our own brains as when we ourselves smile, cry, or bang our shins (although to a lesser extent). Neuroscientists call these *mirror neurons*.[8] Their scientific data confirm that when we see others experiencing happiness or pain, it directly contributes some amount of happiness or pain in our minds as well. This extraordinary (and fairly recent) discovery provides a biological explanation for our tendency to sympathize with others. Our brains seem naturally wired to be empathetic.[9]

Let's explore Pete's empathy toward others and look at a few different ways that helping a stranger might make him feel happy.

Suppose Pete sees a person bundled up in cold weather and feels sympathy for him. So he helps that person by bringing him a cup of hot coffee.

First, since he felt the person's pain, he now also feels a measure of his relief as well. Pete might think, "If I were in his position, I'd want someone to offer me a little bit of help."

Second, by giving happiness to others, Pete might feel happy because his actions remind him of how fortunate he is to be in a better position.

Third, by helping people, Pete might feel a sense of satisfaction because he has been able to make someone else feel happy and enjoys the knowledge that he can effect tangible changes in the lives of others.

Fourth, by helping others, Pete's self-esteem might rise because he can think of himself as a caring person, which is important to his self-image.

Since moral behavior is often defined in terms of acts of selflessness, we can reformulate the traditional view of moral behavior to accommodate personal happiness as follows:

Moral behavior relates to the amount of happiness one person derives from the happiness of another.

A person can be said to act in a moral manner if he or she derives a great deal of self-happiness from other people's happiness. A person acts immorally if he or she derives little self-happiness from the happiness of others or, worse still, derives happiness from the pain of others. With that definition, we remove the requirement of selflessness from morality and focus our attention on what really matters—identification with others and wanting good for them. Giving to charity or helping strangers can still be entirely moral even if you derive happiness from those acts.

The most universally accepted way of thinking about morality is in terms of the Golden Rule: do unto others as you would have them do unto you. In light of our understanding of our preference for happiness, we can now recast the rule as:

Choose to help others find happiness, just as you seek happiness.

But the Golden Rule attempts to tell us what we ought to do. Didn't we just discredit the idea of moral "oughts" since there's no objective moral truth? Yes—but notice that as we've now paraphrased it, the Golden Rule is consistent with choice. We choose to act morally because our personal preferences are to act in that way. And since those personal preferences so often line up with societal morality—because of enlightened self-interest and identification with others—we end up with an uncomplicated conclusion:

We choose to be moral because of the happiness it brings us.

Does choosing not to tell a lie really have anything to do with happiness? Yes. When viewed in light of the many influences in our lives, we can see that there is joy and reward to be gained from telling the truth. It might take the form of feelings of honor, trustworthiness, or sympathy toward those who have been lied to. Or it might be our desire to be seen as an honest person by others.

The idea that morality depends on our view of life-happiness is best explained by the philosopher Jean-Paul Sartre with the famous example[10] of a young man in France during World War II faced with a moral dilemma: stay at home and care for his ailing mother or join the French Resistance and fight the Nazi occupiers. Sartre notes that universal moral and ethical theories are unhelpful in this situation since *both* the options are valid moral choices.

There is no universally correct answer for what that young man "ought" to do. Rather, the decision depends on what the young man views as most valuable. If he stays at home with his mother, he demonstrates that his moral compass prioritizes compassion for the sick and his commitment to his family. If he joins the Resistance, he demonstrates that his moral compass prioritizes bravery, patriotism, and standing up for one's friends, families, and freedom.

The point is that the young man's moral compass, like all of our moral compasses, is determined by his own preferences. If you are the sort of person who is made happy by caring for others, you will be inclined toward a moral perspective that emphasizes looking out for sick people. Alternatively, if you are the type of person who is made happy by your autonomy and freedoms, your moral compass will prioritize standing up for freedoms in the face of oppression. To put it another way, a young man who decides to be a doctor isn't morally superior or inferior to a young woman who decides to become a United Nations peacekeeper. He is simply made happier in the long run by following his preference to practice medicine.

The link between happiness and moral decision-making isn't a new idea. The Greek hedonists of the fourth century BCE, the Epicureans of the first century CE, and the utilitarians of the twentieth century all saw happiness as the greatest moral good, either for the individual or for society. The conclusion we have reached is a little different because we haven't said that pursuing one's life-happiness is inherently moral. Instead, we've concluded that acting out of rational self-interest and identifying with others often leads to moral behaviors. We follow our life-happiness preferences not out of some moral imperative but because that's how we inherently behave. It's not overcoming our nature—it *is* our nature. Subjective ethics frees us from the trap of believing that our own happiness is moral or immoral. Instead, our own happiness is *amoral* and a natural part of the human condition.

Is it rational to believe in our own systems of ethics if our preferences have been so deeply influenced by our upbringings? To answer this, each of us has to decide (regardless of the influence of others) whether our current set of ethics is the best way we know to lead a happy life within society. Much moral wisdom has emerged in human history. Our choice to follow any of these guiding principles is a choice to accept the testimony of other people who have supposedly lived happy lives according to those principles.

Historically, a good deal of morality taught to us by our parents and society is derived from religion. Does it matter if Dad taught us that we should respect others because he believed it was God's will? Isn't the outcome what counts? As adults we can each choose whether or not to follow any particular moral view espoused by religion. In making such a choice, we may believe in respecting people, not for religious reasons but because it makes us happy.

The systems of morals proposed by religions have often been interpreted and modified by society over time. The link between ethics and God has been used by religion both as a source of knowledge and as a way to justify behavior that leads to happiness in societies. But even if we disregard religion or God as an external motivator for morality, there's still no need to disregard many of the reasonable principles religions have developed and practiced to promote happy societies.

It goes without saying that the moral preferences each of us adopts include a strong bias toward the experiences we've encountered in life, including the way we were raised and the culture in which we grew up. If you have been hurt by lying, then truthfulness is likely to be important to you. If you have been praised for helping others, you're likely to place a high premium on that behavior. Family and friends will usually have played a large part in shaping and influencing your perceptions of happiness and, therefore, morals and preferences.

The link between our own morals and our own upbringings is inescapable. Instead of rejecting this as an arbitrary influence, we must accept it as a consequence of subjective morality. Each of our views on morality is inextricably linked to ourselves, our environment, and our own life experiences. However, this shouldn't give us pause. Just as we accept a good moral principle even if it's historically grounded in religion and reject a bad one, so too do we accept the good influences of our background and reject the bad.

THE SEVENTH AND EIGHTH NON-COMMANDMENTS

We've now explored how our subjective moral preferences develop over time, influenced by our upbringing, experiences within society, and personal inclinations. We've also shown that the choice to act morally is compelling when seen through the lens of enlightened self-interest and identification with others. It is time to add these concepts to our Ten Non-commandments:

I. The world is real, and our desire to understand the world is the basis for belief.

II. We can perceive the world only through our human senses.

III. We use rational thought and language as tools for understanding the world.

IV. All truth is proportional to the evidence.

V. There is no God.

VI. We all strive to live a happy life. We pursue things that make us happy and avoid things that do not.

VII. There is no universal moral truth. *Our experiences and preferences shape our sense of how to behave.*

VIII. *We act morally when the happiness of others makes us happy.*

10

SOCIETAL HAPPINESS

Some day you will find out that there is far more happiness in an-
other's happiness than in your own

—Honoré de Balzac

Our focus so far has been on how we individually develop moral preferences and beliefs. We explored how our upbringing, experiences,
and environment can shape our preferences. Now we'll pull back from the
individual to look at society. To do so, we will address a few key questions:

- How do societal ethics develop over time?
- How do individuals reconcile their preferences with the preferences
  of others?
- What role do laws play in the context of societal ethics?

ETHICAL NORMS

In the previous chapter we used the example of Pete to show how a person
forms moral preferences. Pete's moral preferences are a collection of guiding principles based on many influences and experiences he's encountered
in his life, including his upbringing and environment. This collection also
includes a powerful moral driver—deriving happiness from the happiness
of others through enlightened self-interest and identification with others.

Now we'll explore the influence of societal ethics on Pete's moral
preferences. Societal ethics are simply the ethical standards adopted by a
group of people who combine in a society. Let's imagine that Pete lives in

a society with one hundred other people. Pete has his own personal moral preferences, and so does every one of the one hundred other members of this society.

We can simplify this further by pretending that each member of this hypothetical society has only five preferences. Pete's five preferences might include not lying to people he cares about, respecting other people's property, wanting to become wealthy, wanting to have many wives, and wanting an education. Another member of this society, Jennifer, holds a somewhat different set of preferences. Hers might include not lying, not allowing rape, protecting children, wanting to become wealthy, and wanting to enjoy walks in nature.

Given these differences, which no doubt extend across all hundred citizens, what ethical standards might this society adopt as a whole?

There are sure to be some moral preferences that almost all the members of this society can agree on, and also many preferences that fall into the middle ground where there are several supporters but also several opponents. The preferences that are most common and least controversial will be the ones most of the society ends up regarding as personally beneficial.

Let's say one common preference is a desire not to be lied to by others. It would be beneficial for most members of the society to promote this value to others to reinforce and strengthen its influence—not least because a few others might not agree with this value in the first place, and even those who do might decide not to always adhere to it.

So how might members of this society decide to promote such a value? They might tell each other directly how they feel about that value and share anecdotes about the bad things that happened to people when they were lied to. Members might shame and reprimand a person who transgresses or actively spread information about a person's reputation as a liar. They might teach this value directly to children in schools through fables and stories. They might even create laws to punish people who tell particularly destructive types of lies such as libel and slander.

Through these various methods, it soon will become widely known in this society that telling a lie is wrong, and sometimes even criminal.

By doing this, the society will have established an *ethical norm*. A norm can have a strong influence on individuals within a society. Suppose that you are a citizen in this society and didn't originally have the preference for not lying as one of your five moral preferences. You will soon find that when you lie to other people, they rebuke and shun you because truthfulness *is* one of their preferences. It won't be long before you come to realize that by adopting the moral norm of not lying, you can increase your personal life-happiness because other members of the society will treat you better, and you'll feel more socially accepted.

That's how basic ethical norms have emerged. But we're not saying that the majority perspective is automatically moral. After all, a majority of Americans at one point incorrectly thought women should not be allowed to vote. What we are saying is that societal norms can have a great influence on the moral preferences of individuals in any society. This influence, together with a person's upbringing and life experiences, will contribute to the way that person forms moral preferences.

HOW ETHICAL NORMS EVOLVE OVER TIME

Before we explore how members in a society debate ethical perspectives and how we value the strength of one person's perspective to another's, let's explore a little deeper into how ethical norms develop within societies.

Societal ethics are behavioral systems espoused by a group of individuals who combine in a society. As such, they are man-made constructs that reflect the happiness preferences of each person as they relate to themselves and to other members of society. To better understand how these systems emerge, we can draw an analogy with another form of man-made societal construct—systems of government.

Over the centuries, various types of government have been tried as a way to create cohesive societies. For example, since ancient Greece, there have been numerous experiments in democracy—electoral democracies, parliamentary democracies, multiparty democracies, and democratic republics, to name a few. Democracies themselves have evolved over the centuries in response to the many adjustments to the laws and constitutions of these democracies. Today's democracies are the product of much refinement, and they rest on the collective wisdom of many societies, thinkers, and politicians.

Consider for example how democracy in the United States changed the process for electing the vice president. Before 1803, the runner-up in the election of the president became the vice president. In the elections of 1796 and 1800, it became evident that this system had serious flaws—not least that the new vice president was as much an opponent as an ally of the president.

To fix this, the Twelfth Amendment was passed by Congress in 1803, requiring that votes for the president and vice president be distinct. The system evolved even further in 1940 when Franklin Delano Roosevelt became the first presidential candidate to name a running mate before the election. The system we now have in place for electing the president and vice president is the product of adjustments made over more than two centuries in response to flaws in the system.

If we examine the various forms of democracies that have existed, certain concepts have consistently emerged, such as the concepts of tallying votes and collecting taxes. Others vary more widely, such as the role of representatives in government. Compare the presidential republic form of democracy in the United States with the parliamentary form of democracy in the United Kingdom. Both systems tally votes, and both systems tax their populations, but their electoral processes differ. The U.S. president is elected by popular vote, whereas the British prime minister is the leader of the winning party.[1]

When looking at the formation of systems of government, two key insights emerge:

1. Systems of government evolve over time, and
2. They trend toward common practices, such as the collection of taxes.

Let's apply each of these ideas to ethical systems.

Unlike objective moral views, which would remain constant throughout time, subjective ethics evolve in light of the changing viewpoints of the citizens of a given society. At the same time, society's views on ethics have emerged over time through the contemplation and experimentation of many generations of societies and thinkers.

What this means is that modern views about societal ethics don't exist in isolation. Rather, they are the product of observations, trends, and debate over millennia. In the near term, governments evolve when new laws are passed or when new officials are elected. Our happiness preferences may evolve as we experience or learn about new things. So too may commonly accepted ethical standards change over time as people try new things, observe the results of certain systems and behaviors, and embrace new concepts and technologies.

An example of a behavior whose ethical status has seen a dramatic change is slavery, which was commonplace three centuries ago but now is almost universally condemned as unethical. Many advocates for slavery promoted the financial benefits of slave ownership. Others would stand on religious authority and cite Biblical verses such as, "Slaves, obey your earthly masters in everything you do."[2] Over time, the tide turned, and antislavery reformers like William Lloyd Garrison, Frederick Douglass, and Harriet Beecher Stowe were ultimately successful in making the case that we would be better off extending basic human rights to all people. Over time, growing moral and political support for the abolition of slavery persuaded enough Americans, each with his or her own particular experiences and preferences, and the ethical landscape shifted. Eventually the laws themselves were changed to forbid slavery. We can see from this example how societal ethics can evolve over time.

HOW TO DEBATE ETHICS

Now let's look at the way societal ethics trend toward specific practices. Just as features like taxation have become almost universally accepted in democracies of all kinds, certain common features have emerged in societal ethics over time and have become almost universally accepted. For example, it's hard to find a modern society without prohibitions against murder, rape, and theft. While there are significant differences between the ethical frameworks in these societies, all tend to agree that these crimes are unacceptable. Granted, each may have different reasons for holding these positions, but the fact that they all get there one way or another reinforces the validity of these concepts. Despite all the experimentation with ethical frameworks and attempts at living pleasurable lives within societies, no practical ethical system has emerged that negates these basic prohibitions. That's when you know you must be doing something right.

Some people who argue against subjective ethics claim that if ethics are *only* subjective, there's no way to debate ethical standards with others (or, stated differently, that all opinions on ethics would be meaningless). Clearly, this is not the case. The mere fact that our opinions and your opinions are both subjective doesn't mean we can't sensibly debate between the two. Subjective doesn't mean "without reasons." You might just convince us that your reasons are a better fit even for our own self-interests.

Just as we can intelligently and meaningfully debate about different forms of government, we also can thoughtfully discuss different opinions on ethics. While it might be unclear whether a parliamentary system is intrinsically more beneficial to its citizens than a presidential republic, both would seem to be more beneficial than, say, a totalitarian dictatorship or a government that arbitrarily assigns roles via a lottery system.[3]

Sam Harris makes a similar point in his book *The Moral Landscape*, using the example of how we think about food. No one would claim that there must be one objectively correct food to eat. Yet, as Harris explains, we can still discuss the differences between foods, both in terms of their effects on our health and in terms of which foods might taste the best. So why would we think there has to be one objectively correct moral action in any given circumstance for us to have a discussion about morality? Just as there are different tastes in food, so too are there different tastes in morality—even though some may conflict with the collective good.[4] We aren't committing ourselves to the absurd perspective that all moral views are equal, only admitting that there isn't one absolute moral option.

So if we *can* meaningfully debate ethical questions in a society, how do we go about doing so? One path may be discussing the way a given ethical standard is likely to affect the future life-happiness of the members of the society. A discussion of societal ethics is basically a conversation about hypothetical worlds governed by certain principles and rules, one that speculates on how such worlds would appeal to our own happiness and to the happiness of others. We can debate the likely consequences of a particular system and guess which systems would create the greatest life-happiness for people in the society. But we start with a clear assumption that each person wants to live in a society that will enhance his or her own happiness as well as that of others.

You may recall that one of Pete's five desires is to have multiple wives. He mentions this to a few prospective wives and tells them why he thinks this will lead to greater life-happiness for both himself and for them. He tells them of all the joys they can expect to experience being married to him, as well as the shared benefits they can have from multiple mothers looking after their communal children.

The prospective wives beg to differ. They tell Pete that such a concept doesn't appeal to them. They point out to Pete that whenever polygamy has been tried throughout history, it has never turned out very well for the women involved. They tell Pete that, in their opinion, their life-happiness will be most enhanced through a committed, monogamous relationship with a faithful husband. They tell Pete that they have no interest in marrying a man with such antiquated moral preferences. Finally, they tell Pete to "take a hike."

Taken aback, Pete considers his options and the effect they might have on his own life-happiness. He decides he can:

1. Continue to approach other women until he finds some who are more amenable to polygamy.
2. Deceive women into thinking he would be faithful.

3. Move to another society where attitudes toward marriage are different.
4. Actively try to reform his existing society by convincing others of the benefits of polygamy.
5. Change his view of polygamy.

After pondering these various options, Pete realizes that making polygamy a high priority will require him to sacrifice many other happiness preferences. He might have to compromise on the type of women he could be with, because the requirement "fine with polygamy" will seriously reduce the pool of candidates. He might have to compromise on the type of society he'd like to live in.

Ultimately, Pete decides that his personal life-happiness is most likely optimized by repressing his desire to have multiple wives and conforming to the prevailing moral wisdom that monogamous marriages are conducive to optimizing the life-happiness of members of this society.

Is Pete's conclusion reasonable? There's no absolute moral truth to whether monogamy is moral, but there are definitely more or less reasonable perspectives. For example, it would be unreasonable for Pete to espouse polygamy just because he thinks he's a superior lover compared to other males and so has a moral obligation to take multiple wives.

On the other hand, it seems reasonable for Pete to conclude that, although his sexual desires aren't confined to a single woman, the commitment of marriage as understood by other members of society, including the women he would consider marrying, is a commitment to a monogamous relationship.

In other words, we can expect that reasonable people living in a particular society will have certain basic moral preferences. Just because there's no absolute moral code that dictates that murder is unethical doesn't mean that we should be surprised when members of a society raised under similar circumstances come to the common conclusion that murder is immoral.

The basic level of intelligence and social exposure that most kids have by the time they graduate high school would make certain shared moral views pretty likely. We can expect most rational young adults to conclude that murder is bad for societies. Any normally adjusted young adult will have learned enough about the way the world works to recognize and value the desire of others to live their lives unharmed.[5] It's hard to imagine any rational young person, much less an adult, who conceives of a society in which rampant murder would be a benefit. Or, that he or she might be able to convince others that such a society would be an improvement over the one they've got.

Even in a system of subjective morality, certain fundamental morals will emerge almost universally, just as taxation has emerged almost universally in systems of government. This isn't because some absolute order exists in the universe to dictate that it be this way. Rather, it's the product of many rational people in a society who want to maximize their own life-happiness coming to similar reasonable conclusions based on life experiences, the teachings of previous generations, the lessons of history, and the simple benefits that come from societies that promote cooperation.

Of course, so far we've focused our examples on clear-cut ethical issues like murder, rape, lying, and stealing. But a lot of morality falls across a spectrum in which the preferences of individuals are harder to predict. There's no consensus on how much a person ought to donate to charity, for example. And should we regulate people's eating habits with laws such as New York City's effort to ban big soft drink servings or trans fats?

The fact that some issues are less clear doesn't change how we debate societal ethics. It just emphasizes that there are a lot of gray areas created when we try to make sense of the complex balance between our own life-happiness preferences as individuals and the preferences of others.

We should also acknowledge the role of the environment or society in determining what ethical principles people can be expected to adopt. Consider how much easier it is to not steal when you live in a prosperous society where food is abundant. If you live in a deeply impoverished area and are constantly malnourished, you're far more likely to abandon that particular moral principle in the presence of an unguarded loaf of bread.

LAWS AND MORALITY

No discussion about societal ethics is complete without some attention to the role of laws. Certain rules of behavior lead to more productive societies, so societies have decreed that some principles should be explicitly defined and enforced, not just left to the individual to come to rational conclusions. These rules are called *laws*. Laws or legal rules differ from moral rules in that they are narrowly prescribed and defined, and they carry clear penalties for people who violate them. Laws, together with government-sanctioned enforcement structures such as courts, police, and prisons, are used to promote certain types of behaviors and to discourage others.

In most democracies, many of these laws coincide with moral senti-ments and are removed or updated over time as society develops and ethical viewpoints evolve. There's often an interesting time lag between the laws of a society and the moral perspectives of the people living in that society. The members of each generation must assess the laws of the previous gen-eration to decide if they want to continue with the same laws or change them. Consider the evolution of U.S. law with respect to interracial mar-riage. The United States Racial Integrity Act of 1924 banned interracial marriage between white people and black people. After time passed and American attitudes readjusted, the new electorate reconsidered the question and rejected the viewpoints of previous generations.

It's shocking to realize that the interracial marriage of the parents of Barack Obama, the president of the United States at this writing, was illegal in twenty-two U.S. states at the time of his birth.[6]

Laws form a basic framework for the individuals of a society to func-tion collectively. Punitive measures like monetary fines, public shaming, or prison time are designed to influence a person's behavior. These punish-ments would clearly affect a person's perceived life-happiness, so they act as a deterrent.

It's the interplay among laws, societal ethics, and our own life-hap-piness that we contemplate when facing ethical decisions. The choice to be a comparatively moral person is easier in the context of a society with well-considered ethical laws, since breaking these laws will usually fail to optimize a person's life-happiness. In other words, laws often set up an incentive structure that aligns individual self-interest with behavior that benefits society at large.

Modern elected governments adjust to the sentiments of the elector-ate, so over time the laws of these governments tend to line up with the views of the majority and, therefore, with popular ethics. That's not to say that laws are a substitute for morality[7] or that there won't be certain laws that clash with an individual's subjective morals (indeed, both authors of this book oppose the death penalty). But over the long term, the laws of a society tend to correlate with the moral perspectives of the majority. Many of the most fundamental and least controversial morals may well become enshrined as laws, which can make it that much easier for us to choose to act morally.

An area of societal ethics we haven't yet explicitly discussed is how inclusive a society should be. How should we weigh the preferences of the many against the preferences of the few? We'll discuss this in the next chapter.

THE NINTH NON-COMMANDMENT

These discussions about individual and societal ethics help us to better understand why we try to preserve good ethics among the members of society. If those around us behave ethically and predictably, we're in a better position to maximize our own happiness. It's beneficial to us when society preserves and protects a way of life that's conducive to our own contentment. That's why we often reinforce ethical values when we see others straying by chastising or publicly shaming them. As discussed in the game theory example, by reprimanding people who stray, we reinforce the message that cooperation is in everyone's long-term interests. If we all actively work to maintain a society where people behave ethically, we each derive benefits from that society. So it's not only reasonable to be a good person, it's also reasonable to work to create an ethical society.

We can add the notion of collectively promoting ethics within society to our list of Ten Non-commandments:

I. The world is real, and our desire to understand the world is the basis for belief.
II. We can perceive the world only through our human senses.
III. We use rational thought and language as tools for understanding the world.
IV. All truth is proportional to the evidence.
V. There is no God.
VI. We all strive to live a happy life. We pursue things that make us happy and avoid things that do not.
VII. There is no universal moral truth. Our experiences and preferences shape our sense of how to behave.
VIII. We act morally when the happiness of others makes us happy.
IX. *We benefit from living in, and supporting, an ethical society.*

11

PUTTING ETHICAL
BELIEFS TO THE TEST

A good head and a good heart are always a formidable combination.

—Nelson Mandela

A railway trolley has lost its brakes and is hurtling down the railroad tracks. In its path, five people are sitting on the track, tied up and unable to move. The trolley can't be stopped, and the people can't be moved in time.

You are standing next to a junction lever that can send the trolley onto a side track before it hits the people. But wait! There's one person sitting on that side track, eating his lunch. If you do nothing, the trolley will kill five people. If you pull the lever, you will switch the trolley off its current path onto a new path that will result in the death of one person.

What would you do?

THE TROLLEY PROBLEM, FROM
AN OBJECTIVE MORAL PERSPECTIVE

The "trolley problem" is a classic scenario used by philosophers to test ethical concepts.[1] Most people would say it's a no-brainer—pull the lever and save the five people at the expense of one. This is a utilitarian perspective that seeks the greatest good for the greatest number.

Now let's change the scenario. To save the five people, rather than just pulling a lever, you need to physically push a person in front of the trolley to stop it from reaching them. Despite the seeming equivalence in result—one person dies and five are saved—here conventional moral wisdom tends to favor not pushing a person in front of a trolley and allowing the five people to die by inaction, rather than *actively* murdering one person.

Yet, that scenario makes most people deeply uncomfortable, even if they agree with the argument. This moral struggle occurs because people are confronted with a clash of competing principles. For an ethicist who believes in universal moral truth, every action inherently has a morally "correct" way to behave. Pushing a person in front of a trolley conflicts with the absolutist moral view that deliberately killing another individual is morally wrong.

Similarly, there's an absolute moral view that says that saving a person's life is morally right. Even though, in this scenario, the action of pushing a person in front of the train is motivated by the desire to save five other lives, it's mentally challenging to compare two absolutes because it's logically impossible.[2] An absolute principle to not murder an innocent is weighed against an absolute principle to save innocent lives.

The result is an ethical paradox, because absolute principles cannot be negotiated. So doing nothing, which removes the clash of the two absolutes altogether, tends to be the popular choice, even though it results in the maximum loss of life.

THE TROLLEY PROBLEM, FROM A SUBJECTIVE MORAL PERSPECTIVE

By comparison, how would a belief in subjective morality influence your behavior in these trolley problem scenarios? First, you would accept that your actions aren't dictated by a moral absolute. Rather, the choice whether or not to pull the lever is based on your own moral preferences. These include a complex mix of personal experiences and projections of the consequences. Will saving five lives console you from the loss of one life? What does the law say you should do? Could you sleep well at night knowing that you pushed another person in front of a trolley, remembering the look on his face, the sound of his voice crying out?

You'll notice that the trolley description is deliberately devoid of specific personal details. There are people on the track, but not *particular* people. Yet these details may ultimately affect a person's decisions. The *details* are what allow for subjectivity.

- Does the one person appear to be especially worthy of saving?
- Is it my mother?

- Is it a friend?
- Is it the president of the United States (and did I vote for him or her)?
- Will someone see me push the person in front of the train? What would that person think, and what could the consequences be for me?

These are the details that can heavily influence our thinking about how an action or inaction is likely to affect our life-happiness. It would certainly be comforting to answer whether pulling the lever was just right or wrong, like a math problem.

But subjective morality doesn't give us a simple answer—it instead helps us examine our own choices and motives for acting. The better you can think through the options and outcomes of your actions, and the better you can understand your own happiness preferences, the more likely you'll be satisfied with your actions.

Of course all of this individual preference doesn't take place in a vacuum. A system of subjective morality maximizes a person's life-happiness within a society that seeks to do the same. So subjective morals are more concerned with the outcomes of events and the consequences of such events as they relate to oneself rather than absolute moral principles. Someone who believes in subjective morality wants to live a happy life and so cares deeply about how events unfold and the consequences such events could have on his or her personal life.

By the same token, a subjective ethicist might be concerned with different ethical concerns than an objective ethicist. She might worry about the enormous psychological damage and sleepless nights that she'll experience from pushing an innocent in front of the trolley. Or she might be concerned that if she tries to push the other person onto the tracks, that person might resist, and both of them could potentially end up on the tracks in front of the trolley. To avoid any chance of such an outcome, a subjective ethicist might favor doing nothing to avoid the chance of personal harm, psychological or physical. She might also prefer to do nothing to avoid being judged unfavorably by others if they learned that the person who stopped the train was actually pushed in front of it.

That's not to say that inaction is always the favored choice of a subjective moral viewpoint. The subjective nature of these choices means that another person with different subjective moral views might favor saving five lives because of the happiness he or she expects to derive from saving more people—especially if he or she knows the survivors.

If this seems implausible, imagine for a moment that the five people imperiled on the trolley tracks include your mother, father, brother, and child. Suddenly it's easier to understand why you might choose to push a stranger in front of the trolley. Meanwhile, another person might choose to sacrifice himself to save both the stranger and the five people. This example shows how one person might analyze the situation and arrive at a different subjective moral decision than that of another person who is being equally thoughtful.

The subjective element of a person's moral preferences does highlight that most of us will tend to favor people we know and love over strangers. We would look at the trolley track example very differently if we were told that our mothers were imperiled on the train tracks. Similarly, it would be reasonable to expect that a father who sees two children drowning would save his own child first rather than a child he doesn't know. This seems reasonable because intuitively most of us realize that we care much more for people with whom we have existing relationships than we do for strangers.

Through the lens of subjective morality, this attitude seems perfectly reasonable since we expect to derive more happiness from relationships with people with whom we expect to have repeated interactions. Unfortunately, as we all know, this attitude can be taken to extremes in the case of cronyism and nepotism, as well as tribalism and the sad tendency to dehumanize anyone who is different from us.

A subjective perspective doesn't mean there's no reason to care for others unless we have a relationship with them. As we've already discussed, "identification with others" and "enlightened self-interest" can lead us to feel happy when helping others, even if we expect to get nothing tangible in return other than our own satisfaction.

For example, MSNBC host Lawrence O'Donnell has established a charity called the K.I.N.D. fund (Kids In Need of Desks)[3] that provides desks to needy kids in Africa and employs African craftsmen to build those desks. Thousands of American viewers choose to donate money to this charity. Clearly they do so because they derive a sense of happiness from the knowledge that they are helping to improve the school experience of hundreds of African children, even though they are unlikely to personally meet any of the children they are assisting.

Still, on the spectrum of how well we treat other people, we will almost always favor those with whom we have longer-term meaningful relationships. Research as far back as the work of Charles Darwin has shown that we are generally motivated to care more strongly for our families and our close social groups.[4] The circle of caring then radiates outward to include people in our surrounding communities, states, and countries.[5]

Why is this? Why don't we treat everyone exactly the same? It's simple: we invest more energy in relationships that have a higher likelihood of benefiting us than others from which we expect to benefit less. While the ideal of treating every person as if he or she were identical might at first seem an appealing aspiration, it falls apart when we consider real-world practicalities. Parents would be terrible in that role if they neglected their own children's needs to tend to the needs of strangers.

The simple empirical observation is that treating everyone exactly equally is not how we are incentivized to behave by our preference for happiness and the nature of our relationships with other people. Because we depend on some people more than others, they matter more to us, and because others depend on us more than they depend on others, we matter more to them. In the great scheme of things, this isn't a flaw but an evolved feature of the human mind.

The parent-child relationship, the spousal relationship, the caretaker relationship—all are examples of situations and relationships that *require us* to treat the other person in the relationship (the child, the spouse, the sick person) differently from strangers.

A LIST OF ETHICAL QUESTIONS

To move away from the general case and delve into more practical questions about the subjective moral perspective, we need an individual to examine. Once again, we, the authors, have volunteered. This time we will use Lex as the subject and John as the questioner.

We are in no way claiming that Lex's views represent a correct moral perspective. Rather, they are Lex's subjective views based on his specific individual experiences, intellect, and encounters with life. We are mostly interested in showcasing the process around his thinking, and seeing how subjective ethics can be applied.

> *John:* Let's start with a pretty basic moral question. Lex, do you believe it is wrong to murder someone?
>
> *Lex:* Yes, like the vast, vast majority of people in the world, I regard murder as immoral. Let me put it another way: I don't think I'd get any happiness from the act of murder. In fact, I'm certain it would cause me psychological discomfort.

John: Why do you think that?

Lex: Well, empathy, for one thing. I value my own life tremendously, and that makes me feel how strongly others value their own lives. There's also self-interest involved. If murder became acceptable or commonplace, someone would be more likely to kill me, and I'm opposed to that.

John: So does your empathy apply only to humans, or do you believe that killing animals for human consumption is immoral?

Lex: It's an interesting question. I do get happiness from eating meat, and I suppose that joy is more valuable to me than the joy I'd feel from saving the life of a cow. I must admit that even saying that out loud makes me uncomfortable. I had a lot of pets growing up, and I certainly saw them as something more valuable than a meal and do feel empathy toward animals. On the other hand, we also had a lot of Sunday afternoon barbecues, and I enjoy meat . . .

John: So where do you come out on this issue then?

Lex: Ultimately, my preference is to continue to eat meat. I would prefer that animals used for food be treated humanely while they are alive though, so that their suffering is limited to their death. In other words, I don't derive any happiness from the unnecessary suffering of animals prior to being slaughtered. I also choose to eat beef more sparingly because of the effects it might have on my health. I have high cholesterol.

John: Back to people for a minute. Do you believe in sentencing people to death if they have committed murder?

Lex: You mean if they are accused of committing murder. That's part of the problem. But even if someone behaved reprehensibly, I don't expect to get any personal joy from the destruction of that human's life. I've heard a lot of very thoughtful arguments against capital punishment, and as a result I consider it unethical to murder even a murderer.

Even more alarming, the condemned aren't always guilty. There are many cases of wrongful convictions. In the United States, DNA evidence has allowed the exoneration of eighteen death row inmates since 1989.[6] So the small pain I feel in paying a portion of my tax dollars to imprison murderers is less than the larger pain I feel from the knowledge that our society sometimes accidentally kills innocent people.

John: You talk a lot about your preferences and pursuing happiness. Were the Boston Marathon bombers[7] behaving ethically if they were following their preferences?

Lex: Well, first of all the question assumes a false premise. We didn't say that pursuing one's happiness is moral, just that people do, in fact, pursue their happiness. Life-happiness is our main motivation. Morality, on the other hand, is about how much happiness one gets from the happiness of others. The Boston Marathon bombers, Tamerlan and Dzhokhar Tsarnaev, were most likely following their happiness preferences, which valued the advancement of their cause—a deeply misguided form of Islam—ahead of the lives of those affected. But by no means does that equate with morality.

I read about statements one of the brothers wrote on the inside of the dry-docked boat in which he was hiding. They reflect his motivations. He wrote things like, "We Muslims are one body. you hurt one, you hurt us all," and, "Now I don't like killing innocent people it is forbidden in Islam but due to [unintelligible] it is allowed."[8] That second phrase could be appended to many of the most heinous acts of immorality in human history, and the justification is indeed often unintelligible to others.

Acting morally (as we describe in our eighth non-commandment) means deriving happiness from the happiness of others. Clearly the brothers were prepared to inflict pain on others and so acted in an immoral way.

John: How should we think about their motivations then and why they were prepared to harm so many bystanders?

Lex: A system of subjective ethics lets us understand why people like these brothers can end up doing such terrible things. A person's life-happiness preferences can deviate from those held by most people, and a person's conjectures about outcomes can be quite misguided. That's why our society goes to great lengths to outlaw such acts and try to prevent them. The brothers' actions grossly violated basic moral standards commonly accepted across the world to not commit acts of terrorism—the indiscriminate murder of innocent civilians for political or ideological gain.

John: How would you try to convince people like this that their actions are wrong?

Lex: If I had been able to confront the brothers before they acted, I would have tried to reason with them. I would have explained why the bombings would not be in their own self-interest nor in the long-term interest of their cause. I would have walked them through all the possible ramifications of their actions, including the high likelihood that they would be caught or killed. I would have tried to convince them that their worldview—not Islam itself but their view that violence is justified in the name of Islam—is not conducive to creating life-happiness for themselves and the society they live in. I would have attempted to convince them that their extremist Islamic beliefs were in error, and no evidence exists to suggest they would find paradise in heaven. But some people are not willing to listen, and I fear this would be the case in this instance.

John: Let's move on to a very different kind of killing: Do you believe euthanasia is moral?

Lex: I've seen the suffering of elderly and sick people firsthand, including some who were very close to me. This strongly shaped my opinion that even though the preservation of life is generally good, euthanasia is a moral act in certain carefully bounded situations. I sympathize with people who suffer and the pain they have to endure, so I support their desire to end their own suffering, as long as it is their own uncoerced choice and they are of sound mind. Seeing that suffering end would make me happy, even though their deaths would greatly sadden me.

John: I know your background is Jewish—do you believe in the teachings of Judaism?

Lex: I was born and raised as a Jew, but I don't believe the teachings of Judaism that profess to know about the nature of God. I do realize that many of my happiness preferences have been shaped by exposure to Jewish values and culture. I still strongly identify with, and derive happiness from, associating with Jewish culture. I see a vast separation between the cultural aspects of a religion and the faith in its sanctity. I like chopped liver and herring. I like family dinners around the Passover table. I like the Jewish sense of humor and the history of the Jewish people. I am culturally Jewish yet, at the same time, a fervent atheist. And I'm far from alone in those views.

John: So do you think you value living a moral life because of your past exposure to religious values, or is there another reason?

Lex: I choose to live a moral life because of the happiness I expect to derive from living such a life. I take pride in conducting my life in a moral manner and in my ability to derive happiness from the happiness of others. I believe that such a life will lead me toward a rewarding and fulfilling existence. I value living in an ethical society and encourage and promote good behavior among the people with whom I interact. I feel good when my friends think of me as a person of high morals and integrity.

A few patterns emerge from Lex's statements. For one thing, he exhibits a bias toward his personal upbringing and his exposure to liberal Jewish values, as well as his own natural tendency toward gratifying his own desires, coupled with a desire to act rationally.

While his ethical opinions may differ from yours, his ability to answer these questions shows that a person with a subjective ethical perspective can effectively confront the ethical dilemmas he or she might encounter in life. Moreover, he demonstrates that our Ten Non-commandments for the Twenty-first Century do provide the necessary tools and concepts for evaluating ethical situations. We've also seen that moral behaviors can exist within a system of subjective ethics and that a belief in God is not necessary for a person to value moral behavior and strive to be a moral person.

THE FINAL NON-COMMANDMENT

Having subjected our Ten Non-commandments to a system test, we can now say that the framework appears to be coherent, comprehensive, and useful. We can then conclude that the three core assumptions we originally selected appear to be sufficient to form a framework of belief that encompasses beliefs about both facts and ethics.

It's taken a good amount of debate and probing to get us to this conclusion. The whole purpose of this book has been to present and illustrate ways to form, validate, and refine a belief system. A critical element of this process has been testing our beliefs along the way to see if they hold up and remain consistent.

We can then add this essential step—testing, refining, and validating—to our list and finally arrive at the complete list of Ten Non-commandments:

I.   The world is real, and our desire to understand the world is the basis for belief.
II. We can perceive the world only through our human senses.
III. We use rational thought and language as tools for understanding the world.
IV. All truth is proportional to the evidence.
V.   There is no God.
VI. We all strive to live a happy life. We pursue things that make us happy and avoid things that do not.

VIII.   There is no universal moral truth. Our experiences and preferences shape our sense of how to behave.

IX.   We act morally when the happiness of others makes us happy.

X.   We benefit from living in, and supporting, an ethical society.

XI.   *All our beliefs are subject to change in the face of new evidence, including these.*

Now that the list is complete, we can ask: How do these non-commandments stack up against the biblical commandments?

The first four biblical commandments relate to the existence and worship of God. In contrast, the non-commandments have one belief related to the contrary position—the nonexistence of God—and four additional beliefs about the nature of existence and truth in the world.

The remaining six biblical commandments list the moral imperatives to honor our parents and never murder, commit adultery, steal, lie, or covet. The biblical list is woefully incomplete. Why ban coveting your neighbor's property but not ban rape? Why is a ban on lying more important than a ban on slavery? Certainly slavery and rape have inflicted more needless suffering and caused more senseless damage throughout history than lying about your age or wishing your neighbor's new car was yours. Honor your father and mother? What if they're abusive? Don't kill? What if it's in self-defense? Don't steal? What if my family is starving?

In contrast, the non-commandments provide four beliefs about the nature of human behavior, including the formation of morals and the benefits of ethical societies. It provides a holistic framework for evaluating any moral situation, not just a list of selected prohibitions. While having a clean list of dos and don'ts might seem appealing, human life is (fortunately) much too rich and varied for any finite list to govern. It is far better to develop a framework for moral reasoning than rely on the rote ability to follow rules. Our list provides such a framework.

Most importantly, our list includes a belief about the need to test, revise, and edit our beliefs as we gain knowledge or as the culture evolves over time. This stands in stark contrast to the biblical commandments, which are rigid, absolute, and beyond debate or revision. The non-commandments can evolve; the biblical commandments are literally set in stone.

Finally, the non-commandments are beliefs that have been justified and explained. They are beliefs that are accompanied by evidence and rationales. They follow a path of logic with one belief leading to the next and together forming a coherent framework about the world and the people who live within it.

HARMONY, HAPPINESS, AND ATHEISM

The motivation behind this book was to put forth a positive set of carefully considered beliefs consistent with the atheist mind and the humanist heart. While it has taken a fair bit of explaining, the system of belief described and these Ten Non-commandments for the Twenty-first Century have established that you can still hold strong positive beliefs about the world and act morally without any belief in a deity. No assumption of a God is necessary in order to make sense of the world, live in harmonious societies, or achieve happiness.

Negating God does not leave a vacuum of belief—it liberates the beliefs you can hold. Now beliefs can be justified by reason instead of appeals to authority, and they can be tested by evidence rather than being accepted out of faith. Ethics can be debated intelligently rather than imposed. Beliefs can evolve and change over time as we learn and evolve rather than remain rigid dogma.

So we can correct G. K. Chesterton's famous assertion, "When a man stops believing in God, he doesn't then believe in nothing; he believes in anything." Instead, we can say with confidence, "When a man stops believing in God, he doesn't then believe in nothing; all beliefs are instead based on reason and evidence rather than faith."[9]

The benefits of examining those things we hold true, and those we hold good, far outweigh any detriments. Let's work together, led by the thirst for knowledge and the light of reason, to live the best lives we can.

12

FINDING YOUR
OWN NON-COMMANDMENTS

Knowing yourself is the beginning of all wisdom.

—Aristotle

The Ten Non-commandments for the Twenty-first Century we've proposed are our best attempt at putting down on paper the ten most fundamental beliefs we hold. We arrived at these after much time, thought, and debate. We have tried to make our beliefs universally relevant, but we realize that these beliefs, anchored as they are to our own subjective perspectives, come with biases and flaws.

For that reason, we want you to improve on our beliefs and come up with your own. We invite you to correct our errors, overcome our deficiencies, and construct your own "top ten list" of beliefs. We hope your list will prove as useful to you as our list has been to us. The inner resolve, clarity, and comfort that arise from reaching a state of self-understanding cannot be understated.

More than anything, the structured process we followed proved invaluable—perhaps even more so than the set of beliefs we eventually arrived at. This process was based on a few critical principles: writing down your beliefs, building a system from the foundation up, explaining why and how you arrived at each belief, and reaching the essence of your beliefs.

Why is committing your beliefs to paper so important? As noted in the introduction, we discovered an interesting thing while writing this book. We often thought we had a part of the puzzle solved in our minds. It all seemed to make sense while locked up in our heads. But when we wrote it down using language, not thoughts, and read it back to ourselves, we often found issues and flaws.

The exercise of writing down and examining the words, phrases, and logic really does help you understand what you're saying. We have no doubt that as you read this, part of you might think you already have your beliefs all figured out. We challenge you to write them down and see if you still come to the same conclusion or if it leads you to a different result.

Too often when people debate values, beliefs, and morals, they simply talk past each other. The reason is simple: each person is working from different assumptions or fundamental beliefs. Without disclosing what those fundamental beliefs are, people approach things from different angles and so don't understand why they can't make sense of each other's views. By writing down your beliefs, you gain clarity on what your core beliefs and assumptions really are.

Finally, by writing it down, you'll be confronted by the words staring back at you. This is very powerful. Are those *really* your core beliefs? Writing them down means mentally committing to them. They will be recorded in time with the weight and consequence of history. You can return to them later to see what has worked and what hasn't, and you'll be able to see how your thoughts have changed over time.

Revising your core beliefs is part of the process of making them better and stronger. But before you can revise, you have to record your first version. Committing them to the page also makes the fifth and final step of the scientific method possible: sharing your thoughts with others so they might offer a constructive critique and help you refine your views. It can also encourage and inspire them to engage in their own thoughts. So we invite you to a dialogue about what's truly important in life and what you really believe about knowledge, reality, and ethics.

Why is it so necessary to build a belief system from the foundation up? If we were put on the spot and asked what we believe in strongly, most of us could list a few principles we hold dear. But these are often just a list of strong opinions that don't form a comprehensive system of belief. A simple way of thinking about the foundation-up approach is to think of the list as a prioritized list. If one belief comes ahead of another, it means that the first belief is more fundamental than the later one and is required in order to arrive at the subsequent belief. Prioritizing beliefs facilitates a holistic systems approach and reduces the likelihood of ending up with a list of logically disconnected or inconsistent statements.

Why should each of your beliefs be justified and explained? For non-believers, justification and evidence are essential. A rejection of God is almost always driven by a search for evidence for God's existence that ended in a fundamental lack of such evidence. Any new belief system that is not to be rejected for the same reason has to provide support for its propositions. The same drivers behind the atheist mind—critical thinking, clear reasoning, and explicit justification—dictate that we follow these very principles when constructing a new system of belief. Beliefs without clear justification are arbitrary, and any alternate belief would be equally valid.

Why is reaching the essence of your beliefs important? Distilling your ideas facilitates clarity and allows you to get to the heart of what you really believe. It's been said that you can't fully comprehend something until you can say it in its simplest terms. Ten beliefs might seem an arbitrary number, but it does force you to distill your concepts and sharpen your views.

As we've said and shown throughout the book, there's good evidence to favor simplicity. A crystallized list of ten beliefs in short sentences and clear language helps promote that simplicity. If you come up short at nine beliefs, or run a little long with eleven, that's fine by us. Inspired by our belief that "brevity is the soul of wit,"[1] we think that ten non-commandments should give you sufficient form to spell out your own views while remaining brief enough to be easily read and understood by another person.

We've offered some principles for constructing the framework. Here's a set of proposed guidelines for the actual process:

1. Write down your beliefs.
2. Order the beliefs by importance.
3. Explain why and how you arrived at each belief.
4. Try to think of counterexamples to your beliefs. Test out your beliefs in practice.
5. Show your list to friends who are interested in the subject to get feedback.
6. Revise or re-explain as your ideas evolve.

We would further recommend a stylistic approach of structuring your beliefs so that the first group of beliefs relates to the nature of existence, truth, and facts, and the second group relates to human behavior, morals, and ethics.

Don't be intimidated by the process. Just start by generating your first potential belief. Then ask yourself the question, "Why do I believe in that?" Whatever your answer, ask yourself again why you believe *that* particular answer and how it satisfies the question. Keep following this iterative process of asking yourself *why?* until you reach a belief that is so fundamental and core to your worldview that no other beliefs can be used to justify it. You'll know you're there when you run out of answers and are left with something like, "I don't fully know why logic works, but I can't conceive of a world without it." *Boom*. That's the sound of hitting bedrock—a source belief.

After arriving at your source beliefs, continue to derive and build additional beliefs until you arrive at a comprehensive framework. Throughout the process, just like a curious young child, keep asking yourself that very simple question: *why?*

Here are a few questions that were useful to us in our journey. Perhaps they can help you jump-start your own thought process:

- How do you justify your beliefs?
- Do you believe in the value of science as a means of inquiry?
- How do you define facts or truth?
- Do you believe in God? What type of God?
- How should you behave?
- How do you define morality?
- Do you believe in a universal moral truth?
- Can you describe the ideal society that you would like to live in?

Now it's time to commit your beliefs to paper. We hope your journey through these pages will have brought you closer to already knowing many of your own answers. We encourage you to borrow and steal from us, but never accept anything on our authority. Instead, always ask yourself why you believe what you believe. We also encourage you to reshape our list in your own way, to reject our views as needed and start afresh. And, of course, we encourage you to reflect, debate, and ponder.

Our list took us several years of thinking, many months of writing, and pages of explanations. We hope our example will make the process easier for you. Even if you can't yet get clarity on all your beliefs, perhaps you can start with just the first one. Write it down. Let it germinate, and come back to it. Maybe it will change. Maybe it will lay the foundation for the next belief.

For your convenience, we've provided a template, which follows. (We completed this same template for our Ten Non-commandments in appendix B.) Copy this template or use it as a guide in creating your own non-commandments. You can also download the template from our website. Better still, at our website you can post your version online to share your ideas with others and become part of a grand dialogue to discover what to believe. Visit us at www.AtheistMindHumanistHeart.com.

Good luck, and have fun!

MY TEN NON-COMMANDMENTS
AS WRITTEN BY _____ ON _____

I.   _____

II.   _____

III. _____

IV. _____

V.   _____

VI. _____

VII. _____

VIII. _____

IX. _____

X.   _____

JUSTIFICATIONS AND EVIDENCE TO
ACCOMPANY MY TEN NON-COMMANDMENTS

I. _____

_____

_____

II. _____

_____

_____

III. _____

_____

_____

IV. _____

_____

_____

V. _____

_____

_____

VI. _____

_____

_____

VII. _____

_____

_____

VIII. _____

_____

_____

IX. _____

_____

_____

X. _____

_____

_____

_____

Appendix A

COMMON RELIGIOUS OBJECTIONS

The truth springs from arguments amongst friends.

—David Hume

Earlier in this book we used a core concept to conclude that God does not exist—that no reliable means exists to determine the relative validity of the various descriptions of God. So believing that any one view of God happens to be the correct one, and that (in most cases) it happens to have been the one you were born into, is equivalent to believing you hold a winning lottery ticket before the results are announced. This is playing the "religious lottery."

Four common objections are often raised by religious believers to discredit this analogy. The first is the unified theory of God, which argues that the apparent perceptions of different gods are really just different views of the same God. As a result, goes the reasoning, there are millions of winning lottery tickets, so you probably *are* holding a winner.

The second objection uses a pseudoprobability argument known as Pascal's Wager, which claims that since the jackpot is so large—a place in heaven—and the cost of the ticket is so small, the mathematics of probability dictate that you should buy a ticket just in case.

A third reason provided for a belief in God is evidence in the form of miracles. Miracles take the form of events that contravene the laws of nature and, therefore, are used to show that some other being must exist beyond the boundaries of the natural. Some religious believers even claim to have directly observed God, heard his voice, or seen his image.

Finally, the fourth reason is psychological comfort. Some proponents of a belief in God say that while they acknowledge that there is no evidence for God's existence, we should nevertheless believe in God because of the social benefits and psychological comforts such a belief provides. A belief in God gives us hope, makes our suffering in the world more tolerable, and motivates people to be moral.

We will address each one of these pro-God arguments in turn: the unified view of God, Pascal's Wager, miracles, and psychological comfort.[1]

A UNIFIED VIEW OF GOD

Many liberal, spiritual, or nondenominational believers hold the unified view of God, where the gods being worshipped by the various religions are actually the same singular God. Philosopher of religion John Hick explains this unified theory of God and why contradicting claims of various religions might exist by drawing an analogy to the parable of the blind men and the elephant, often attributed to the Buddha:

> An elephant was brought to a group of blind men who had never encountered such an animal before. One felt the leg and reported that an elephant is a great living pillar. Another felt the trunk and reported that an elephant is a great snake. Another felt a tusk and reported that an elephant is like a sharp ploughshare. And so on. And they all quarreled together, each claiming that his own account was the truth and therefore all others false. In fact, of course they were all true, but each referring only to one aspect of the total reality and all expressed in very imperfect analogies.
>
> Now the possibility, indeed the probability, that we have seriously to consider is that many different accounts of the divine reality may be true, though all expressed in imperfect human analogies, but that none is "the truth, the whole truth, and nothing but the truth." May it not be that the different concepts of God, as Jahweh, Allah, Krishna, Param Atma, Holy Trinity, and so on . . . are all images of the divine, each expressing some aspects or range of aspects and yet none by itself fully and exhaustively corresponding to the infinite nature of the ultimate reality?[2]

The pluralistic view of God has three main flaws. First, it ignores the problem that certain descriptions of God directly conflict with each other. If two blind men were both feeling the same tusk, and one claimed that the tusk was soft and the other that it was hard, even with a larger knowledge about an entire elephant, the blind men could not both be correct.

In reality, views of God by the various religions do often propose directly contradictory views. Christians believe Jesus is God. The Jewish view holds the inverse—that this same Jesus is not God. No matter how you look at the big picture, both these views of God cannot be true—only one can be true, or neither.

The second main flaw with a pluralistic view of God is that it does not specify what to exclude. It assumes that all the blind men are touching and describing an elephant. What if one blind man was instead touching a giraffe, another was touching a bear, and only the third was touching an elephant? The parable assumes that the elements being described are connected, but they might not be. The assumption that all versions are automatically correct is the least likely and least satisfactory of all.

The third flaw with a unified view of God is that it misses what the religious views of God actually are. Different religions do not claim only to have some vague notion of God. Rather, each religion affirms that its particular beliefs directly reflect the will of God himself. For example, Judaism believes that the words of the Bible are the precise words of God. The Bible is not claimed to be a vague description written by some blind man about his experiences with some God. On the contrary, the core of Jewish belief is that God himself gave the Bible to humankind. To continue the analogy, here the "elephant" wrote its own description of what it is and gave it to the blind men.

Most religions derive their doctrines from God directly—which is why religions profess to know the truth, not merely a part of the truth. If we reject the claim that the Bible was given to humankind by God, there is simply no reason left to believe that the Bible explains "the truth" because it has no divine source. It is for these reasons that David Hume famously asserted "that, in matters of religion, whatever is different is contrary."[3]

PASCAL'S WAGER

We have relied heavily on the laws of probability to demonstrate that holding a particular view of God when faced with so many equally plausible views of God is not rational. But probability too has been used to propose a counter argument for a belief in God—the most noteworthy being Pascal's Wager, which can be summarized as follows: as long as there is some small positive probability that God exists, it follows, since infinity multiplied by any finite amount generates an infinity, that the expected utility of believing that God exists swamps that of disbelief.[4]

The argument here is that no matter how small one takes the odds to be that God exists, the act of believing that God exists carries an infinite expected utility (eternal afterlife). Thus one could maximize one's potential outcome simply by believing rather than disbelieving.

While Pascal's argument purports to show that probability could be used to justify a belief in God, on closer examination several flaws become apparent.

One problem is that Pascal assumes that belief in a certain religion definitely leads to infinite bliss. But religions frequently damn each other mutually, so it's equally possible that believing in a religion that turns out to be false could send a person to one of the various hells that have been imagined. Furthermore, if we accept Pascal's way of thinking, we could use it to justify *any* behavior, as demonstrated by the following extreme, but still relevant, example:

> Either (a) there is a God who will send you to heaven only if you commit a painful ritual suicide within an hour of first reading this, or (b) there is not. We cannot settle the question whether (a) or (b) is the case. . . . But (a) is vastly preferable to (b), since in situation (a) infinite bliss is guaranteed, while in (b) we are left in the usual miserable human condition. So we should wager for (a) by performing the suicidal ritual.[5]

As soon as we remove unfounded assumptions about the qualities of God (such as only granting eternal bliss), Pascal's argument can be used to condone *any* action—even suicide.

MIRACLES AS EVIDENCE OF GOD'S EXISTENCE

Some theologians cite miracles as evidence for the existence of God. These most often come in the form of human testimony of either direct communication with God or witnessing miracles performed by God. Miracles in the Old Testament include God's creation of a fire in a bush that never burned,[6] God stopping the sun in the sky for Joshua to do battle,[7] and, in the New Testament, Jesus walking on water.[8]

Modern-day "miracles" include accounts of terminally ill patients surviving a disease or infertile couples becoming pregnant. In India, Hindu swamis claim to perform miracles such as turning barren lands into forests. These miracles are typically explained as spectacular manifestations of God's direct intervention to alter the laws of nature to promote a divine plan (oftentimes brought about through prayer).

First let's examine the eyewitness accounts of people who claim to have witnessed miracles. Human testimony is a form of information we encounter routinely in our lives when evaluating what to believe. Based on our prior experience with the accuracy of various sources of information, we choose to classify sources based on our perception of their trustworthiness. Human testimony is no different. We also evaluate the content of the testimony by comparing it to knowledge we may already have from our own direct observations or from other sources.

How should we establish the credibility of witnesses who claim to have seen violations of the laws of nature in the form of miracles? The philosopher David Hume, who dealt extensively with the topic in his essay *On Miracles*, suggests the following method for evaluating testimony about miracles:

> No testimony is sufficient to establish a miracle, unless the testimony be of such a kind, that its falsehood would be more miraculous, than the fact, which it endeavours to establish. . . . When anyone tells me, that he saw a dead man restored to life, I immediately consider with myself, whether it be more probable, that this person should either deceive or be deceived, or that the fact, which he relates, should really have happened. I weigh the one miracle against the other; and according to the superiority, which I discover, I pronounce my decision, and always reject the greater miracle. If the falsehood of his testimony would be more miraculous, than the event which he relates; then, and not till then, can he pretend to command my belief or opinion.[9]

In other words, we should evaluate any testimony about a suspension of the laws of nature against the testimony of the laws of nature itself and decide which is more probable. The regularity of nature is itself a proof. Laws of nature are laws that have repeated themselves endless times without alterations. We should only believe in the account of a miracle if it would be more miraculous that the person giving the account was in error, than that the miracle itself did not occur.

Let's apply Hume's procedure to the miracle in the book of Joshua when the sun is said to have stood still for one day while the Amorites were conquered by Israel.[10] In deciding whether to believe such an account, we should compare the evidence in favor of such a belief with the evidence against it.

The evidence against the biblical story is its inconsistency with Newtonian physics, which does not allow for the sun to stand still. Newton's laws have been substantiated by countless observations and tests. The evidence for a belief in the biblical story is, of course, that the Israelites testified to having seen the sun stand still. We need to compare the two forms of evidence and determine which would be the greater miracle—that the witnesses were deceived or that the laws of nature were suspended.

Since humankind is fallible and is often deceived, it seems more probable that the witnesses were somehow mistaken than that the laws of nature were invalidated.

The credibility of witnesses to ancient biblical miracles is further undermined by the limited knowledge these witnesses possessed to understand what they might have been observing. To believe in biblical miracles on account of human testimony is to believe in the credibility of a people who lived in an age when the sun was still thought to orbit the Earth and there was no significant knowledge about chemistry, electricity, optics, or medicine.

To cast even more skepticism on these witnesses, even the people in the Bible who testified to some of the miracles were not completely convinced by what they supposedly saw. The Egyptian pharaoh needed to see ten miracles to be convinced. The Israelites, after being led through the miraculous splitting of the Red Sea, still were not convinced enough to refrain from worshiping the golden calf. If these miracles offer such clear evidence for a belief in God, why were they not sufficient to convince the very people who witnessed them to become believers?

Finally, there is the issue of the intermediary, the author of the text itself. It's possible that no such testimony was ever made by the Israelites because the story itself was entirely fabricated by the author—not necessarily to deceive but as a teaching fiction, a common practice of the time.

Thankfully the progression of knowledge, science, and education over the last five thousand years has led to a precipitous decline in the number of alleged accounts of the spectacular type of miracles found in the Bible. What some people class as "miracles" today, such as a terminally ill patient surviving a disease or infertile couples becoming parents, tend to be descriptions of outlier occurrences with extremely low probability that nonetheless occur rather than fantastic revelations by God that defy nature.

These outlier events push the limits of our understanding of nature, but they do not offer any credible evidence for any God. Applying the principle of favoring simplicity (Ockham's razor) to these events, we should pick the explanation that is the simplest and contradicts existing knowledge the least. Believing that a supernatural realm exists is a far more complex explanation than believing that these events are statistical outliers or that our own scientific understanding of disease or fertility has limits.

In summary, the very limited and often questionable evidence of eyewitness accounts of God or miracles provides a very weak justification for a belief in God. When compared against the standards of evidence used to support scientific beliefs—which include concepts such as empirical observations; repeatability; and double-blind, randomized studies—the evidence for God is not at all compelling. It is for this reason that so many religious believers do not cite miracles as a justification for their belief. Rather, they say they believe in God out of *faith*. God is an assumption, not a deduction.

PSYCHOLOGICAL COMFORTS OF BELIEVING IN GOD

Some proponents for a belief in God argue that there is a psychological benefit to faith. They argue that a belief in God provides us with comfort and hope. In times of hardship and sorrow, God can give people a way to cope with the suffering in the world and with difficult realities such as death. A belief in God, it is said, motivates us to be moral and creates more manageable societies. Religion just feels good.

The Judeo-Christian religions portray a God who is a father figure who will look out for you and protect you from the cruelty and injustices of the world. Another analogy used in the Bible is God as a shepherd looking out for the safety of his flock. "I am the good shepherd: the good shepherd giveth his life for the sheep."[11]

We can distill these pro-God arguments into two types:

1. Belief in God is comforting.
2. Belief in God is useful for creating harmonious, productive societies.

If we try to cast these arguments in the most favorable light possible within the framework of our non-commandments, we get:

1. Since a belief in God provides us with happiness, we can choose to believe in God for the happiness it will provide.
2. Belief in God is a tool used to promote ethics and harmony in a society.

We will address each of these two arguments.

Can one choose to believe something one knows to be untrue? Let's say you have one hundred dollars in your bank account. It would be much more comforting for you if you had ten thousand dollars in your account instead. That would allow you to worry less about making ends meet and paying your rent. Could you decide to believe that you actually had ten thousand dollars in your account rather than one hundred?

This is not the way our brains function. Our rational brains can't willfully deceive themselves into ignoring information we know to reflect reality. There's a major difference between hope and belief. Hope is the desire for the world to be a certain way. Belief is one's best assessment of the way the world is. So it would be quite reasonable for you to hope that you will one day have a larger bank balance. But it would be quite unreasonable for you to try to pay for an item at the store with money you know you don't have.

To quote philosopher Sam Harris: "Beliefs are intrinsically epistemic. They purport to represent the world as it is."[12] Harris makes the point that we are slaves to evidence and live under the lash of historical opinion. "Choosing beliefs freely is not what rational minds do."[13] We do not have the ability to choose to believe in a false God, even if such a belief would provide us with additional comforts in life. If we could shape our beliefs based on the comforts they might yield, why would we not believe that each of us is God? Surely being God would be more comforting than needing to be saved by God.

Proponents of this position muddle arguments. They talk of the benefits a belief in God might provide without asking if such a belief is valid in the first place.

A rational mind cannot trick itself into believing something that does not reflect the reality of the world unless the person hasn't made an effort to discern that reality—something even rational people do at times. In that case, no trick is required. Beliefs are simply inserted into a space left empty by a lack of effort. But as you quickly learn when you try to spend that money you don't have, it's always better to operate with as accurate a picture of reality as possible. And even though we can never prove with certainty that God does not exist, we can achieve a high level of confidence on the question.

As discussed in chapter 4, belief in a God is highly irrational because it is playing the "religious lottery" and because there is no evidence to support the existence of such a deity. So regardless of one's hopes for such a supreme being to exist, or for such a being to have qualities and powers that would be comforting, the rational mind cannot help but accept that there is no evidence for such a perspective.

A stronger form of this pro-God argument is that human minds are psychologically incapable of dealing with the notion of death, the randomness of tragedies that might befall us, or the cruelty of human suffering.

The only way to deal with these stark realities is to invent a psychological construct that allows us to pretend we are immune.

Again, a mind that is thinking rationally will not engage in such willful, self-inflicted deception. Moreover, such thinking ignores the reality that there are many, many happy atheists (such as ourselves) living pleasurable, meaningful, and joyous lives every day without any such belief in God.

The second major reason for promoting the belief in God for psychological reasons is the claim that such a belief benefits society because it leads to a happier, more ethical, and more harmonious population. Plato made a similar argument in *The Republic*. After describing his version of an ideal society, he offers his belief that the rulers of such a society must tell "noble falsehoods" to the common people to ensure harmony and to keep them in line. So too do some proponents of God argue that a belief in God is necessary for the greater good of society.

There are several weaknesses to this argument. First, there are numerous historical cases where religion has led to terrible barbarism and cruelty in the world—the Crusades, the Inquisitions, Islamic jihads, the list goes on and on. It seems that a belief in God can just as easily be used to channel hate, anger, and murder as to channel love and compassion.

The converse argument—that the least religious countries in the world are consistently the happiest, most stable societies—is yet another challenge to the assumption that societal happiness and belief in God are highly correlated.

Supporting information for our position comes from the Legatum Institute, a London-based policy advocacy organization that publishes an annual index of "net happiness"[14] using traditional economic indicators as well as measurements of well-being and life satisfaction. The Gallup Organization's annual look at the stated importance of religion in the lives of people in various countries also shows that countries with extremely low religiosity dominate the top ten in societal happiness. In Norway, the consistent front-runner in happiness, 80 percent of the residents say religion is not important in their lives.[15] Sweden and Denmark, currently fourth and sixth in happiness, are also both above 80 percent. Not one of the ten happiest countries has a population in which more than a third of the people say religion is important in their lives.

Another problem with the "noble falsehood" argument is the consequences of false hope. Giving someone false hope is fundamentally about lying to a person. That can turn out to be quite cruel if the person ultimately discovers that he or she has been deceived. Some health clinics have at times claimed their expensive treatments might cure cancer, for example, but when hopes are dashed, the results are often public controversy and legal actions.[16]

False hope can lead to unintended consequences, which can harm people just us much as they are intended to help them. A young family faced with an emergency medical situation for their infant might believe it is more important to take their child to a church to be baptized instead of to a hospital to be saved.[17]

Ultimately, the idea that a belief in God is a "noble falsehood" is deeply condescending and paternalistic. It has a hidden supposition that religious leaders know what is best for the common masses, who cannot be trusted to deal with real knowledge or to make decisions and choices for themselves.

The truth is that we can be trusted with real knowledge and are capable of making our own choices about how to use the information we acquire to inform our decisions. Even more than that, we are better served by a realistic appraisal of reality than by fantasy, no matter how comforting, and should strive to see that reality as clearly as possible. When the English philosopher Francis Bacon said "knowledge is power,"[18] he meant quite literally that knowledge of reality empowers us in a way comforting fantasy never could.

Appendix B

OUR TEN NON-COMMANDMENTS

TEN NON-COMMANDMENTS
FOR THE TWENTY-FIRST CENTURY

I. The world is real, and our desire to understand the world is the basis for belief.

II. We can perceive the world only through our human senses.

III. We use rational thought and language as tools for understanding the world.

IV. All truth is proportional to the evidence.

V. There is no God.

VI. We all strive to live a happy life. We pursue things that make us happy and avoid things that do not.

VII. There is no universal moral truth. Our experiences and preferences shape our sense of how to behave.

VIII. We act morally when the happiness of others makes us happy.

IX. We benefit from living in, and supporting, an ethical society.

X. All our beliefs are subject to change in the face of new evidence, including these.

JUSTIFICATIONS AND EVIDENCE TO
ACCOMPANY OUR TEN NON-COMMANDMENTS
FOR THE TWENTY-FIRST CENTURY

Here is a condensed set of justifications for our Ten Non-commandments—the "nutshell" assumptions and methodology that underlie each conclusion. Each numeral signifies the corresponding non-commandment:

I.   We assume the world is real because, in practice, we all conduct our lives as if the world is not purely a mental construction.

II.   We assume that our five senses are our best chance to accurately perceive reality, because no other reliable sources have been discovered to gather information about the world.

III. We assume that we can trust in language and thought because without them we would have no means of communicating about the world.

IV.   Truth is proportional to the evidence because our observations, coupled with the scientific method, are good at predicting future events.

V.   There is insufficient evidence for a belief in God. Believing in any particular god is playing the "religious lottery."

VI.   We believe that we seek things that make us happy because introspection about our thoughts and desires, and observations of others, are consistent with this perspective.

VII. There is insufficient evidence for objective moral truth. On reflection, our views of right and wrong are inextricably linked to what sort of people we want to be, our past experiences, and the cultural norms of the times.

VIII. We observe that people we consider more moral tend to derive more happiness from making other people happy.

IX.   Ethical societies benefit everyone because it is easier to live a happier life when you are surrounded by other people who value cooperation and take pleasure in your happiness. This is a mutually beneficial relationship.

X.   Beliefs are subject to revision because the more experiences you have in life, the more data you have to draw on, and the more likely you are to formulate accurate conclusions.

Appendix C

THEOREM OF BELIEF

This appendix summarizes the propositions presented in the book in a structured, simplified outline. The intent is to clearly articulate the links between various ideas and the flow of arguments used throughout the text.

Including such transparency and a clearly articulated logic structure is rare in philosophical books of this nature because it is exceptionally difficult to do. But we believe that it is an invaluable step in constructing a ground-up system of belief and has kept us intellectually honest. We hope it will help you recognize the underlying rational structure of this book and the care that has gone into formulating it. We also hope that others wiser than us will read through it, find errors or make suggestions, and collectively help us advance our understanding of how we might best formulate accurate beliefs.

WHAT CAN I BELIEVE?

- *If*

  a belief can only be justified by another belief (P_1)

  then

  starting beliefs cannot be justified (P_2)

  To make starting beliefs nonarbitrary

  i) we can call starting beliefs starting assumptions, *and* (P_3)

  ii) starting assumptions can be validated by system-testing once our system has been put in place (P_4)

- *If*

  we require starting assumptions   *(from P_3)*

  let us assume (P_5)

  i) the existence of an external reality, *and* (P_6)

  ii) trust in our five senses (flawed and limited as they are) for perceiving reality, *and* (P_7)

  iii) trust in language, logic, thought, and the intellect as tools for analyzing and describing reality (P_8)

  and let us define

  truth as an accurate description of the external reality (P_9)

- *If*

  i) we trust in our five senses for perceiving reality, *and*   *(from P_7)*

  ii) truth is an accurate description of the external reality   *(from P_9)*

  then

  we can make observations about truths in the reality (P_{10})

- *If*

  we trust in logic for describing reality   *(from P_8)*

then

we can trust in mathematics and the laws of probability *(P_{11})*

- *If*

  i) we make observations about truths, *and* *(from P_{10})*
  ii) we trust in mathematics and the laws of probability *(from P_{11})*

  then

  we can infer beliefs about the probabilities of future events from multiple past observations, which is inductive reasoning *(P_{12})*

- *If*

  i) we trust inductive reasoning as a tool for discerning truth, *and* *(from P_{12})*
  ii) the scientific method is a formalized method of inductive reasoning *(P_{13})*

  then

  we can trust the scientific method as a tool for discerning truth *(P_{14})*

- *If*

  i) we trust in inductive reasoning as a tool for discerning truth, *and* *(from P_{12})*
  ii) inductive reasoning is based on a person's past experiences, *and* *(P_{15})*
  iii) different people have different experiences *(P_{16})*

  then

  beliefs of observational truth are based on subjective experiences *(P_{17})*

- *If*

  i) we infer beliefs about probabilities of future events from past observations, *and* *(from P_{12})*
  ii) truth is an accurate description of the external reality *(from P_{9})*

  then

  beliefs are probabilistic approximations of truth *(P_{18})*

- *If*

  i) beliefs of truth are based on subjective experiences, *and* *(from P_{17})*

     ii) people's sets of experiences change over time,   *(P$_{19}$)*
     and

     iii) beliefs are probabilistic approximations of   *(from P$_{18}$)*
     truth, *and*

     iv) more data are more representative of reality   *(P$_{20}$)*

then

     i) people's beliefs can change over time, *and*   *(P$_{21}$)*
     ii) their assessment of truth can improve over   *(P$_{22}$)*
     time

- *If*

     i) we trust in mathematics and the laws of   *(from P$_{11}$)*
     probability, *and*

     ii) the probability of multiple beliefs all being   *(P$_{23}$)*
     true is never greater than the probability of just
     one of those beliefs being true

then

     a theory dependent on a larger number of beliefs   *(P$_{24}$)*
     is less likely to be true than one based on a
     smaller number of similarly probable beliefs,
     which is Ockham's razor

- *If*

     we trust in mathematics and the laws of   *(from P$_{11}$)*
     probability

then

     it would be an inaccurate view of reality to   *(P$_{25}$)*
     believe you hold a winning lottery ticket
     before the results are announced, which we
     call the folly of the lottery ticket

- *If*

     i) we can trust our five senses for perceiving   *(from P$_7$)*
     reality, *and*

     ii) our senses have not perceived God's existence,   *(P$_{26}$)*
     and

     iii) Ockham's razor is a useful tool for evaluating   *(from P$_{24}$)*
     multiple hypotheses, *and*

     iv) believing in God is dependent on a   *(P$_{27}$)*
     large number of other beliefs such as the
     supernatural and violating the laws of physics,
     and

v) there are an infinite number of qualities a (P_{28})
supernatural God could possess, *and*

vi) believing in any particular quality out of an   *(from P_{25})*
infinite set of qualities would be equivalent to
the folly of a belief in a winning lottery ticket
choice

then

there is no basis for a belief in God (P_{29})

- *In summary, we can use the following framework for forming* (P_{30})
  beliefs of truth:
    i) we trust in inductive reasoning, *and*   *(from P_{12})*
    ii) we trust in the scientific method, *and*   *(from P_{14})*
    iii) Ockham's razor is a useful tool for evaluating   *(from P_{24})*
    multiple hypotheses, *and*
    iv) beliefs are based on subjective observational   *(from P_{17})*
    experiences, *and*
    v) beliefs are probabilistic approximations of   *(from P_{18})*
    truth, *and*
    vi) beliefs change over time, *and*   *(from P_{21})*
    vii) beliefs become more accurate over time, *and*   *(from P_{22})*
    viii) there is no basis for a belief in God   *(from P_{29})*

- *If the above framework when tested*
    i) has no internal contradictions, *and* (P_{31})
    ii) makes useful predictions about reality (P_{32})
  then
    i) we can accept the starting assumptions as valid, (P_{33})
    and
    ii) we can accept the framework for forming (P_{34})
    beliefs of truth about reality as valid

- *If*
  we accept the framework for forming beliefs of   *(from P_{34})*
  truth about reality as valid

  then

  we can answer the question, "What can I (P_{35})
  believe?" by referring to the framework for
  forming beliefs of truth about reality.

HOW OUGHT I BEHAVE?

- *If*

    I "ought" behave in an objectively correct way (P_{36})
    then
    there exists an objectively correct way for me to (P_{37})
    behave, which we will call *universal morality*
    and let us define
    moral truth as an accurate description of that (P_{38})
    universal moral reality

- *If*

    we accept our earlier framework for forming   *(from P_{34})*
    beliefs of truth about reality
    then
    we can use the framework to evaluate the (P_{39})
    existence of a universal moral reality

- *If*

    i) we trust our five senses for perceiving reality,   *(from P_7)*
    and
    ii) our senses have not perceived the existence of (P_{40})
    a universal morality, *and*
    iii) there is an infinite number of potential (P_{41})
    universal moral codes, *and*
    iv) believing in any particular moral code out   *(from P_{25})*
    of an infinite set of moral codes would be
    equivalent to the folly of a belief in a winning
    lottery ticket choice
    then
    there is no basis for a belief in a universal moral (P_{42})
    reality

- *Even though there is an infinite number of potential universal*   *(from P_{41})*
    moral codes, let us consider the two general categories they
    commonly fall under:
    i) decreed by God (such as religious codes), *or* (P_{43})
    ii) decreed by humans, *whether by:* (P_{44})
       a) a leader appealing to authority (P_{45})
       (such as the Code of Hammurabi), *or*
       b) a philosopher appealing to reason (P_{46})
       (such as Kant, Bentham, or Rawls), *or*

c) the consensus of a population (P_{47})
(such as the moral zeitgeist), *or*
d) the notion of duty (P_{48})

- If
  there is no basis for a belief in God   *(from P_{29})*

  then
  there is no basis for a belief in a universal moral (P_{49})
  reality decreed by God

- If
  i) any particular universal morality decreed by a (P_{50})
  human is influenced by past experiences, *and*
  ii) past experiences are subjective   *(from P_{17})*

  then
  any universal morality decreed by a human is (P_{51})
  inherently subjective and so not objectively
  correct

- If
  i) there is no basis for belief in a universal moral   *(from P_{42},*
  reality, *and* P_{49}, P_{51}*)*
  ii) universal morality is defined as an objectively   *(from P_{37})*
  correct way to behave

  then
  there is no basis for belief in an objectively (P_{52})
  correct way to behave

- If
  we trust in thought and the intellect for   *(from P_{8})*
  describing reality

  then
  we can trust in introspection as a form of (P_{53})
  personal observation

- If
  i) we trust in introspection as a form of personal   *(from P_{53})*
  observation, *and*
  ii) my own introspection has led me to believe (P_{54})
  that I possess the ability to make choices, *and*
  iii) my observations of others are consistent with (P_{55})
  them being able to make choices, *and*

$iv)$ human beings share similar biological characteristics (P_{56})

then

people, in general, possess the ability to make choices (P_{57})

- *If*

$i)$ there is no objectively correct way for people to behave, *and* *(from P_{52})*

$ii)$ people possess the ability to make choices *(from P_{57})*

then

people's behavior is determined by their subjective choices (P_{58})

- *If*

$i)$ we trust in introspection as a form of personal observation, *and* *(from P_{53})*

$ii)$ my own introspection has led me to believe that I am motivated by the pursuit of life-happiness, *and* (P_{59})

$iii)$ my observations of others are consistent with them being motivated by the pursuit of life-happiness, *and* (P_{60})

$iv)$ human beings share similar biological characteristics *(from P_{56})*

then

human behavior, in general, is motivated by the pursuit of life-happiness (P_{61})

where

life-happiness is the predicted sum total of happiness over one's lifetime (P_{62})

- *If*

$i)$ people possess the ability to make choices, *and* *(from P_{57})*
$ii)$ human behavior is motivated by the pursuit of life-happiness *(from P_{61})*

then

people choose to pursue life-happiness (P_{63})

- *If*

life-happiness is the predicted sum total of happiness over one's lifetime *(from P_{62})*

then
life-happiness is based on predictions of how (P_{64})
much happiness we will derive from future
events

• *If*

i) life-happiness is based on predictions of how   *(from P_{64})*
much happiness we will derive from future
events, *and*
ii) we infer beliefs about future events from past   *(from P_{12})*
observations

then
life-happiness is based on past observations (P_{65})

• *If*

i) life-happiness is based on past observations, *and*   *(from P_{65})*
ii) beliefs of observational truth are based on   *(from P_{17})*
subjective experiences, *and*
iii) people's sets of experiences change over time   *(from P_{19})*

then
i) life-happiness is based on subjective (P_{66})
experiences, *and*
ii) people's knowledge about their life-happiness (P_{67})
changes over time

• *If*

i) people are motivated by the pursuit of life-   *(from P_{61})*
happiness, *and*
ii) cooperation increases an individual's life- (P_{68})
happiness in certain circumstances

then
people are motivated to cooperate in certain (P_{69})
circumstances (even when trying to optimize
their own life-happiness)

• *If*

i) we trust in introspection as a form of personal   *(from P_{53})*
observation, *and*
ii) my own introspection has led me to believe (P_{70})
that I usually feel empathy with others, *and*
iii) my observations of others are consistent with (P_{71})
them usually feeling empathy with others, *and*

    iv) human beings share similar biological   *(from P_{56})*
        characteristics

then

    people usually feel empathy with others   *(P_{72})*

• *If*

    i) cooperation increases one's life-happiness in   *(from P_{68})*
        certain circumstances, *and*

    ii) cooperation by definition benefits multiple   *(P_{73})*
        people, and therefore increases others' life-
        happiness, *and*

    iii) people usually feel empathy with others, *and*   *(from P_{72})*
    iv) empathy implies that experiencing an increase   *(P_{74})*
        in someone else's life-happiness causes a feeling
        of happiness in oneself

then

    increasing the life-happiness of others   *(P_{75})*
    increases one's own life-happiness in certain
    circumstances

• *If*

    we observe that people we consider more moral   *(P_{76})*
    seem to derive more happiness from increasing
    the happiness of others

then we can define

    i) morality as the extent to which increasing the   *(P_{77})*
    life-happiness of others increases one's own life-
    happiness, *and*

    ii) moral behavior as behavior that increases the   *(P_{78})*
    life-happiness of others

• *If*

    i) people are motivated by the pursuit of life-   *(from P_{61})*
    happiness, *and*

    ii) increasing the life-happiness of others increases   *(from P_{75})*
    one's own life-happiness in certain circumstances

then

    people increase the life-happiness of others in   *(P_{79})*
    certain circumstances

• *If*

    i) people increase the life-happiness of others in   *(from P_{79})*
    certain circumstances, *and*

ii) moral behavior is behavior that increases the life-happiness of others   *(from P$_{78}$)*

then

people behave morally in certain circumstances   *(P$_{80}$)*

- *If*

  i) people behave morally in certain circumstances, *and*   *(from P$_{80}$)*

  ii) human behavior is determined by subjective choices   *(from P$_{58}$)*

  then

  people choose to behave morally in certain circumstances   *(P$_{81}$)*

- *If*

  i) ethical societies promote moral behavior, *and*   *(P$_{82}$)*

  ii) moral behavior is behavior that increases the life-happiness of others, *and*   *(from P$_{78}$)*

  iii) an individual stands to benefit when members of a society attempt to increase the life-happiness of others   *(P$_{83}$)*

  then

  ethical societies stand to increase the life-happiness of their members   *(P$_{84}$)*

- *If*

  i) ethical societies stand to increase the life-happiness of their members, *and*   *(from P$_{84}$)*

  ii) people are motivated by the pursuit of life-happiness   *(from P$_{61}$)*

  then

  people stand to benefit from living in an ethical society   *(P$_{85}$)*

- *If*

  i) supporting an ethical society increases the likelihood of the society being ethical, *and*   *(P$_{86}$)*

  ii) people stand to benefit from living in an ethical society   *(from P$_{85}$)*

  then

  people stand to benefit from supporting ethical societies   *(P$_{86}$)*

- *In summary, we can use the following framework for forming* (P_{87})
beliefs of ethics:
    i) there is no basis for a belief in a universal   *(from P_{42})*
    moral reality, *and*
    ii) people choose to pursue life-happiness, *and*   *(from P_{63})*
    iii) life-happiness is based on subjective   *(from P_{66})*
    experiences, *and*
    iv) people's knowledge about their life-happiness   *(from P_{67})*
    changes over time, *and*
    v) moral behavior is behavior which increases the   *(from P_{78})*
    life-happiness of others, *and*
    vi) people stand to benefit from living in an   *(from P_{85})*
    ethical society, *and*
    vii) people stand to benefit from promoting   *(from P_{86})*
    ethical societies

- *If the above framework, when tested,*
    i) has no internal contradictions, *and*   *(from P_{31})*
    ii) makes useful predictions about people's (P_{88})
    behavior
then
    i) we can still accept the initial starting (P_{89})
    assumptions as valid, *and*
    ii) we can accept the framework for forming (P_{90})
    beliefs of ethics as valid

- *If*
    we accept the framework for forming beliefs of   *(from P_{90})*
    ethics as valid
then
    we can the answer the question, "How ought (P_{91})
    I behave?" by referring to the framework for
    forming beliefs of ethics.

ACKNOWLEDGMENTS

What a journey writing this book has been since we first put down on paper the simple question, "What should I believe?" We are extremely grateful for those who have helped along the way, providing support, advice, and thoughtful commentary.

Our largest thank-you goes to our editor, Dale McGowan. Dale has been a delight to work with. He has helped make our ideas that much more readable, accessible, and engaging. His dedication to our efforts and sincere interest in our message have been remarkable. We have learned so much from Dale about the craft of writing and storytelling.

Several other writing professionals have assisted in polishing the messages of the manuscript and contributing ideas at various times along its development, including Mike S. Malone, Lydia Bird, James O'Shea Wade, Barbara Egbert, and Bjorn Carey. Thank you for your contributions.

Several readers from the atheist, humanist, and agnostic community have read versions or parts of the manuscript at different times. Thank you to Peter Boghossion, Steven Wissing, Brentney Hamilton, and David Fitzgerald for taking the time to provide us with comments and insights.

Finding a publishing partner for two first-time authors on a controversial subject such as atheism took persistence. Many thanks to Sarah Stanton at Rowman & Littlefield for recognizing the potential of our book and embracing our message and vision. Thank you also to Tom Krattenmaker for the initial introduction.

We often worked on the book in coffee shops. Overhearing our discussion, patrons would frequently come over and share their opinions, which made us realize how important these issues are to so many people. As the book makes its way to press, we see this as the beginning of a dialogue with readers. You are welcome to join that dialogue at www.AtheistMind HumanistHeart.com.

LEX BAYER

A special thanks goes out to my brother, Ross. Thank you for countless Sunday brunches over the last several years spent engaging and debating the ideas of the book and being such a constructive sounding board. I am grateful for the time you spent reading, rereading, and commenting on so many different forms of the manuscript. In the section on logic, your input was invaluable. I still smile when I think of how much fun we had together in our sessions attempting to grapple with the myriad references and cross-references that make up the logic section. Thank you for embracing my crazy audacity of trying to wrestle such big metaphysical ideas into clear and precise statements. I learn so much from you every time we are together. Your mind can be even more rational than mine, and your heart . . . well, it is far bigger as well.

I want to thank my sister, Kelly, who is an inspiration to me in all things. Her support throughout my life is something I cherish dearly and a source of endless joy. I could not wish for a better sibling.

My mother has been a fountain of support over my lifetime. She dedicated much of her life to ensuring that, as a child, I had every opportunity to learn, grow, and succeed in whatever I did. I am ever grateful for her endless encouragement and resolve. She raised me to dream to do big things.

Candid feedback is something I value so dearly in life, and I am grateful to the people who take the time and emotional energy to provide it. Many friends were gracious enough to read versions of the book, provide comments and suggestions, or engage with me over certain ideas. Thank you to Tom, Dave, Kirsten, Adrienne, Julie, Jonny, Shelly, Onn, Sylvia, Joe, Atiya, and Vanessa. Several friends provided support, encouragement, and counsel along the way. In particular, I would like to thank Greg Smith and Adrienne.

It's powerful to look back on one's life and pay tribute to certain individuals who were able to change one's life outlook in profound ways and enrich it forever. I pay tribute to my high school English teacher, Digbi Ricci, who instilled in me an appreciation for literature, language, and intellectual ideas. Indeed, it was Digbi who first quoted Chesterton to me on hearing that I was a nonbeliever. Little did he know the long-winded response he would evoke.

I owe a tremendous debt to the institution of Stanford University. What a remarkable, inspirational, and empowering place. Not only did Stanford fund most of my education but it broadened my mind in so many ways. As an incoming freshman narrow-mindedly focused on becoming an engineer, I rolled my eyes at the prospect of needing to complete mandatory requirements in the humanities and writing. I was looking forward to getting through these requirements as quickly and efficiently as possible. I had signed up for the history track, but in a stroke of luck I didn't get my first choice and was forced to take the philosophy track instead. Little did I know how much the study of philosophy would grab my interest and resonate with me. Trying to make the most of my mandatory freshman writing class, I decided to write about my views on religion. There I discovered the value of open-ended writing as a tool for discovery, and it gave me the confidence to write more.

JOHN FIGDOR

First, I would like to thank my parents, without whose support I couldn't have completed this project. From reading to me from as early as I can remember to investing in my education and encouraging my intellectual pursuits to supporting me in my darkest moments, you've been the best parents I could hope for.

Second, I have to thank all of my teachers, from my K–12 education in Scarsdale Public Schools to my professors at Vassar and Harvard Divinity School to my colleagues at Stanford. Philosophy is the practice of standing on the shoulders of giants. You are the giants who have allowed me to become the philosopher and religious studies scholar I am today. I would like to particularly thank Professors Doug Winblad and Jeffrey Seidman from Vassar's Philosophy Department, Professor Alexei Klimoff from Vassar's Russian Studies Department, Professor Dudley Rose from Harvard Divinity School, Professor Richard Parker (Christopher Hitchens's college roommate) from Harvard's Kennedy School of Government, and Professor Philippe Van Parijs from Harvard's Philosophy Department.

Third, I would like to thank the authors who broke the silence and made it possible for atheists and humanists to write books such as this one: Richard Dawkins, Sam Harris, Daniel Dennett, and the late Christopher

Hitchens. I spent an enormous amount of my time at Harvard studying, learning about, and debating the material of these four authors. Their dedication to clarity of thought and their willingness to engage reasonably and responsibly with their critics has been an inspiration. Additionally, I'd like to thank Hemant Mehta, David Fitzerald, Greta Christina, Richard Carrier, James Croft, Greg Epstein, Steven Pinker, Rebecca Goldstein, Bart D. Ehrman, William Rowe, Peter Singer, Ron Giere, Galen Strawson, Hillary Bok, Judith Jarvis Thompson, and the late Douglas Adams and Jorge Luis Borges for all that I have learned from you.

Last, I would like to thank Rev. P. Washburn for my early education in religion and Rev. Jim Wallis and Rev. Arthur G. Broadhurst for reminding me that some humanists choose to call themselves Christians.

NOTES

INTRODUCTION: QUESTIONING EVERYTHING

1. "It is the custom on Erev Yom Kippur to ritually slaughter a white rooster during the morning 'watch' after Selichot, for then a thread of divine grace prevails in the world. We slaughter it to subdue the supernal severities, and take out its blood to 'sweeten' the severities. It is called Kapparah (expiation), as was the scapegoat. Each member of the household should have a Kapparah—a rooster for each male and a hen for each female. A pregnant woman should have three fowls: a hen for herself, and a rooster and a hen for the unknown gender of the child. . . . [I]n the second paragraph, turn the chicken around your head (for a total of nine rotations)." *Machzhor for Yom Kippur, with English Translations* (Brooklyn, NY: Merkos L'Inyonei Chinuch, 2004), 2.

2. From *The Laughing Prophet: The Seven Virtues and G. K. Chesterton* (Methuen & Co. Ltd, 1937) by Émile Cammaerts, in which he quotes Chesterton and is regarded as the source of the Chesterton attribution.

3. Will Durant, *On the Meaning of Life* (New York: Ray Long and Richard Smith, 1932).

4. As an example from *Theological and Halakhic Reflections on the Holocaust* by Bernhard H. Rosenberg and Fred Heuman (New York: KTAV Publishing, February 1991, 121): "The Zionists were responsible for the tragedy of the six million. The arrogance of nationalist self-destruction in trying to build a Jewish state caused the great destruction. The fact that so many Zionists were secularists, nonbelievers, only made matters worse. They violated the injunction to remain passive, refrain from interfering in the divinely preordained plans of redemption, and to await the miraculous coming of the messiah. Hence, the Zionists are guilty, and all the Jewish people suffered because of their sins."

5. "God thundereth marvellously with his voice; great things doeth he, which we cannot comprehend" (Job 37:5).

6. Some Christian apologists argue that it is impossible for God to do evil be-cause God defines good by his actions. These Christians believe that God and good are identical, and that whatever God does, whether it is allowing the slaughter of millions in the Holocaust in recent history or killing every living thing that didn't get a Noah's Ark ticket, is moral just by definition. Plato neatly dismantled this absurd argument in his dialogue *Euthyphro*.

7. There are thirty-six chaplains listed on the Harvard Chaplains website, which can be found at http://chaplains.harvard.edu/people.

CHAPTER 1: REWRITING THE TEN COMMANDMENTS

1. A phrase made popular by the cosmologist and astrophysicist Carl Sagan (1934–1996).

2. "I count myself in category 6, but leaning towards 7—I am agnostic only to the extent that I am agnostic about fairies at the bottom of the garden." From Richard Dawkins, *The God Delusion* (Boston: Houghton Mifflin, 2006), 51. In an interview on the television show *Real Time with Bill Maher* (April 11, 2008) Dawkins goes on to clarify that he would describe himself as a 6.9 on the scale.

3. "Very low probability, but short of zero. De facto atheist. 'I cannot know for certain but I think God is very improbable, and I live my life on the assumption that he is not there.'" Also: "We are all atheists about most of the gods that human-ity has ever believed in. Some of us just go one god further." Both from Dawkins, *The God Delusion*. Dawkins promotes self-identification as an atheist with his "Out Campaign," which includes atheist-branded apparel. See http://outcampaign.org.

4. "And the Lord said unto Moses, Come up to me into the mount, and be there: and I will give thee tables of stone, and a law, and commandments which I have written; that thou mayest teach them." Exodus 24:12, King James Version.

5. American Humanist Association, http://americanhumanist.org/Human ism/Humanist_Manifesto_I, http://americanhumanist.org/Humanism/Human ist_Manifesto_II, and http://americanhumanist.org/Humanism/Humanist_Mani festo_III.

6. International Humanist and Ethical Union, http://iheu.org/humanism /what-is-humanism. A lengthier version by the IHEU is "The Amsterdam Decla-ration." See http://iheu.org/humanism/the-amsterdam-declaration.

7. Penn Jillette, *God, No! Signs You May Already Be an Atheist and Other Magical Tales* (New York: Simon & Schuster, 2012).

8. George Carlin, *When Will Jesus Bring the Pork Chops?* (New York: Hyperion Books, 2005).

9. Christopher Hitchens, "The New Commandments," *Vanity Fair*, April 2010.

10. Unless otherwise indicated, all biblical quotations throughout this book are referenced from the King James Version of the Bible.

CHAPTER 2: THE PARADOX OF BELIEF

1. Though often credited to Bertrand Russell, the story predates his birth in one form by more than forty years. It is credited to the Rev. Joseph Frederick Berg in Theodore Parker's *Great Discussion on the Origin, Authority, and Tendency of the Bible between Rev. J. F. Berg, D.D. of Philadelphia and Joseph Barker of Ohio* (Boston: J.B. Yerrington & Son, 1854), 48.

2. Kenneth Appel and Wolfgang Haken, "Every Planar Map Is Four Colorable," parts 1 and 2, *Illinois Journal of Mathematics* 21, no. 3 (1977): 429–90, 491–567.

3. Georges Gonthier, "Formal Proof: The Four-color Theorem," *Notices of the American Mathematical Society* 55 (2005): 1382–93.

4. Does the fact that Ockham's razor is being used as a guide mean that it is necessarily a source belief? No, it is merely a guiding principle. If Ockham's razor can be later deduced from the source beliefs as a derived belief, the system can remain coherent, and no contradiction would exist. We'll see in later chapters whether the system proposed validates the use of Ockham's razor.

5. Another major problem here is that the assumption itself (that the consequences would be terrible) is often demonstrably false.

6. The philosophical term for such a view is "realism."

7. While we believe that there is an external reality, it doesn't particularly matter if we are correct about the ultimate metaphysical *nature* of that reality. For example, it could be the case that we are all minds in a computer simulation of the universe (as popularized in the film *The Matrix*), and that there is no actual "external" reality beyond the structure of the simulation itself (meaning reality is a matter of bits and bytes instead of atoms and molecules). Even if this were the case, we would find ourselves in the same position we are in now. Ultimately, our senses are our only mode of access to reality, whether that reality is properly external or a computer simulation.

8. The comedian Tim Minchin cleverly mused about such a scenario in his beat poem "Storm." The poem portrays a dinner party guest named Storm who confronts Minchin by declaring, "You can't know anything. Knowledge is merely opinion." Minchin's desired retort is "to ask Storm whether knowledge is so loose-weave, of a morning, when deciding whether to leave her apartment by the front door or a window on the second floor." http://www.timminchin .com/2011/04/08/storm.

9. Bertrand Russell, *The Problems of Philosophy*, 2nd ed., introduction by John Skorupski (Oxford: Oxford University Press, 1998).

10. This is the fundamental concept of the philosophical school of thought known as empiricism.

11. This is the traditional list of five senses. Our bodies have additional physiological senses that would be included in a more complete list of biological senses. Examples include the ability of our inner ears to perceive balance or detect acceleration and senses in the skin that can detect temperature.

CHAPTER 3: THE REASONING BEHIND REASON

1. David Hume discusses this example about the belief that the sun will rise tomorrow in *An Enquiry Concerning Human Understanding* (New York: Oxford University Press, 1999).

2. Like the table example in chapter 2, this example is discussed extensively in Bertrand Russell's work *The Problems of Philosophy* (Oxford, UK: Oxford University Press, 1953).

3. This concept is referred to in philosophy and statistics as Bayesian probability.

4. The Innocence Project, "Eyewitness Misidentification," http://www.inno cenceproject.org/understand/Eyewitness-Misidentification.php.

5. A rough estimate of the world population over the last two millennia times 365 days per year of seeing the sun rise times the average lifespan in years.

6. Thomas Nagel, *The View from Nowhere* (New York: Oxford University Press, 1986).

7. Ronald N. Giere, *Scientific Perspectivism* (Chicago: University of Chicago Press, 2006).

8. Peter Godfrey-Smith, *Theory and Reality: An Introduction to the Philosophy of Science* (Chicago: University of Chicago Press, 2003).

9. Jeneen Interlandi, "An Unwelcome Discovery," *New York Times*, October 22, 2006.

CHAPTER 4: BELIEFS ABOUT THE UNKNOWN

1. Isaac Newton, *Sir Isaac Newton's Mathematical Principles of Natural Philosophy and His System of the World*, trans. Andrew Motte (Berkeley: University of California Press, 1960), 398.

2. The Pepper's Ghost effect is an optical illusion that depends on plate glass and mirrors. It causes objects to seem to appear or disappear, or to transform or morph into other objects. The best-known examples are the illusory ghosts in the Haunted Mansion ride in Walt Disney World and Disneyland.

3. California Lottery, http://www.calottery.com/Games/MegaMillions/How ToPlay/FAQ.htm.

CHAPTER 5: THE ASSUMPTION OF A GOD

1. Or, put differently, is God all-knowing, all-powerful, and perfectly good?

2. Thomson Reuters, *Inside the iPhone Patent Portfolio,* September 2012.

3. Michael Jordan, *Dictionary of Gods and Goddesses*, 2nd ed. (New York: Facts on File, 2004).

4. Lynn Foulston and Stuart Abbott, *Hindu Goddesses: Beliefs and Practices* (Eastbourne, UK: Sussex Academic Press, 2009).

5. Some religions do make predictions about the future that can then be assessed for accuracy. Alas, none of these predictions has so far turned out to be accurate. Unfortunately, few religious leaders follow the example of Vietnamese cult leader Hon-Ming Chen, who predicted that God would appear on channel 18 across the United States at 12:01 a.m. CST on March 25, 1998. When the time came and went with no appearance by God, Chen denounced his own beliefs and told his followers to abandon him.

6. This idea was satirized brilliantly in the television show *South Park*. In episode 10 of season 4, several thousand people die and arrive at the gates of hell. Surprised to be in hell, one person asks: "Well, who was right? Who gets into heaven?" The hell director responds: "I'm afraid it was the Mormons. Yes, the Mormons were the correct answer."

7. Pew Research Center's Forum on Religion and Public Life, "Global Christianity: A Report on the Size and Distribution of the World's Christian Population," December 19, 2011.

8. Pew Research Center's Forum on Religion and Public Life, "The Global Religious Landscape: A Report on the Size and Distribution of the World's Major Religious Groups as of 2010," 2012.

9. Exodus 3:2.

10. Joshua 10:13.

11. Exodus 14:21–22.

12. Matthew 14: 22–33.

13. John 11:1–46.

14. This does not include Deists, who believe that the only property of God is the creation of the universe (or setting the cosmological constants that made possible the existence of the universe). Deists do not believe that God intervenes in the world and do not have any specific other beliefs about God's attributes.

15. Blaise Pascal, *Pensees*, trans. A. J. Krailsheimer (London: Penguin, 1966).

CHAPTER 6: PUTTING FACTUAL BELIEFS TO THE TEST

1. This example is discussed by Michael Shermer in his book *The Believing Brain: From Ghosts and Gods to Politics and Conspiracies—How We Construct Beliefs and Reinforce Them as Truths* (New York: Times Books, 2012).

2. We recommend John Perry's *A Dialogue on Personal Identity and Immortality* (Indianapolis: Hackett, 1978).

3. The ship of Theseus, also known as Theseus's paradox, asks whether an object that's had all of its components replaced is still the same object. The paradox asks whether a ship which was restored by replacing each and every one of its wooden parts remained the same ship or was just a copy of the original ship.

CHAPTER 7: FROM BELIEFS TO BEHAVIOR

1. This principle is referred to by philosophers as "psychological egoism."

2. Jeremy Bentham, *The Principles of Morals and Legislation* (Buffalo, NY: Prometheus Books, 1988), 1. Bentham was by no means the first to address the question. In his *Nicomachean Ethics*, Aristotle asked, "What is the ultimate purpose of human existence? What is that end or goal for which we should direct all of our activities? Everywhere we see people seeking pleasure, wealth, and a good reputation. But while each of these has some value, none of them can occupy the place of the chief good for which humanity should aim. To be an ultimate end, an act must be self-sufficient and final, that which is always desirable in itself and never for the sake of something else" (1097a, 30–34).

3. This is consistent with the standard psychological model espoused by the philosopher David Hume, as well as Herbert Simon's "bounded rationality" model.

4. R. A. Wise and P. P. Rompre, "Brain Dopamine and Reward," *Annual Review of Psychology* 40 (February 1989): 191–225.

5. Elizabeth A. Phelps, "Emotion and Cognition: Insights from Studies of the Human Amygdala," *Annual Review of Psychology* 57 (2006): 27–53.

6. Elizabeth A. Phelps, "Human Emotion and Memory: Interactions of the Amygdala and Hippocampal Complex," *Current Opinion in Neurobiology* 14, no. 2 (2004): 198–202.

7. John Campbell Oman, *Mystics, Ascetics, and Saints of India* (London: T. Fisher Unwin, 1905).

8. Randi Fredricks, *Fasting: An Exceptional Human Experience* (San Jose, CA: All Things Well Publications, 2013).

9. David A. Leeming, Kathryn Madden, and Stanton Marlan, eds., *Encyclopedia of Psychology and Religion* (New York: Springer, 2009).

CHAPTER 8: HOW "OUGHT" ONE BEHAVE?

1. Walter Mischel, E. B. Ebbesen, and A. R. Zeiss, "Cognitive and Attentional Mechanisms in Delay of Gratification," *Journal of Personality and Social Psychology* 21 (1972): 204–18.

2. W. Mischel and R. Metzner, "Preference for Delayed Reward as a Function of Age, Intelligence, and Length of Delay Interval," *Journal of Abnormal and Social Psychology* 64, no. 6 (1962): 425–31.

3. We couldn't. Even if we harnessed every CPU in existence, this would still not be possible given the complexity of the problem. But let's pretend.

4. An average human body is estimated to be composed of approximately 7×10^{27} atoms. See Robert A. Freitas Jr., *Nanomedicine* (Austin, TX: Landes Bioscience, 1999). Accounting for the larger size of typical basketball players, ten players on the court, the ball, the court, the hoops, and the air in the stadium easily brings

us to a lowball estimate of 10^{30} atoms involved in a basketball game. The numbers get even more absurd if you include the number of collisions that would be constantly happening between all these atoms every second of the game.

5. Sean Carroll, "Free Will Is as Real as Baseball," *Discover Magazine* (blog), http://blogs.discovermagazine.com/cosmicvariance/2011/07/13/free-will-is-as-real-as-baseball/#.UjyLCn_B_Sh.

6. One of the stranger implications of objective morality is that moral facts existed before any creatures existed that could follow those moral laws and will persist even after those creatures go extinct. As a result, a belief in objective morality means that there were moral laws before there was an earth or even a universe in which these laws could exist and that these moral laws would continue to exist even after the earth ceases to exist. As a result, objective morality tacitly depends on a supernatural lawgiver to provide the laws or the belief that objective morals are themselves supernatural and can exist both before and after the universe came to be.

7. Even if objective moral truths exist, what if human beings don't have a way to perceive them? For example, many people who believe in moral truths don't think that animals experience morality in the same way we do. As a result, when a male lion jumps on a female lion and bites the back of her neck during coitus, we don't describe that as "rape." We also don't draw the conclusion that because lions don't perceive rape as immoral, we shouldn't either. So not only does the moral objectivist have to assume that eternal moral truths exist apart from nature, he also has to assert that we have a reliable way of perceiving and evaluating those moral truths.

8. Richard E. Creel, *Philosophy of Religion: The Basics* (Hoboken, NJ: Wiley-Blackwell, 2013).

9. Ronald L. Eisenberg, *The 613 Mitzvot: A Contemporary Guide to the Commandments of Judaism* (Rockville, MD: Schreiber, Shengold, 2005).

10. Louvre, *Law Code of Hammurabi, King of Babylon*, http://www.louvre.fr/en/oeuvre-notices/law-code-hammurabi-king-babylon.

11. W. W. Davies, trans., *The Codes of Hammurabi and Moses with Copious Comments, Index, and Bible References* (Cincinnati: Jennings and Graham, 1905).

12. Dawkins discusses the moral zeitgeist in detail in chapter 7 of *The God Delusion* (Boston: Houghton Mifflin, 2006).

13. It's an arresting thought to realize that many of the behaviors we hold as neutral or good today may be seen as obviously immoral in later eras: "Can you believe that people back in the twenty-first century didn't allow children to work until they were sixteen? Parents gave them set incomes called 'allowances.' And they kept animals imprisoned in their homes for their own entertainment, giving them demeaning slave names like Mr. Sprinkles!"

14. Steven Pinker, *The Better Angels of Our Nature: Why Violence Has Declined* (New York: Viking, 2011).

15. John Stuart Mill, *Utilitarianism* (London: Parker, Son, and Bourn, 1863).

16. Immanuel Kant, *Groundwork for the Metaphysics of Morals*, ed. and trans. Allen W. Wood (New Haven, CT: Yale University Press, 2002).

17. John Rawls, *A Theory of Justice* (Cambridge, MA: Harvard University Press, 1971). Rawls's philosophy was greatly inspired by Kant.

18. Even a partial list of a few of the dizzying diversity of proposed moral codes would include Kantianism, Neo-Kantianism, Rule Utilitarianism, Act Utilitarianism, Aristotelian Virtue Ethics, Rawlsianism, Care Ethics, Social Contractarian, Communitarianism, and many more.

19. We are not using duty in Kant's technical sense but, instead, in the colloquial sense of the term.

20. "Duty," *Random House Dictionary* (New York: Random House, 2012).

CHAPTER 9: MORAL HAPPINESS

1. William James, "The Will to Believe: An Address to the Philosophical Clubs of Yale and Brown Universities," *New World* (June 1896): 7.

2. While it may seem obvious, it's important to note that Pete wouldn't have any opinion of cheesecake if he hadn't been exposed to it. This is most obvious when Western children are exposed to Indian, Chinese, and Japanese foods for the first time. The more experiences you have, the more freedom you have. It is unfortunate but true that children born in better socioeconomic circumstances often have more freedom than less privileged children as a result of wealthy parents' ability to expose their children to more experiences. While wealthy parents can't necessarily guarantee that their child will pick up piano or fall in love with international travel, children whose parents aren't wealthy enough to provide them access to experiences such as trips around the world or expensive musical instruments simply won't be exposed to those experiences. Fortunately, technology can help us by driving down the costs of certain experiences. For example, while a child may not be able to visit the Louvre, he or she can see the paintings on the Internet and read articles about them on Wikipedia. Organizations such as the Khan Academy democratize knowledge by making school lessons available to anyone with an Internet connection. While the technological proliferation of knowledge and learning is by no means a panacea, it offers new vistas of experience to people who otherwise wouldn't have access to those experiences.

3. These two concepts (identification with others and enlightened self-interest) are explored in Peter Singer's book, *How Are We to Live: Ethics in an Age of Self-Interest* (Amherst, NY: Prometheus Books, 1995).

4. This type of behavior is also often called "reciprocal altruism."

5. For a more comprehensive discussion of game theory, we highly recommend the chapter "Tit for Tat" in Singer's *How Are We to Live?* as well as Bruce Bueno de Mesquita's book, *The Predictioneer's Game: Using the Logic of Brazen Self-Interest to See and Shape the Future* (New York: Random House, 2009).

6. The societal desire to keep track of how people behave has resulted in systems designed specifically for this purpose, such as permanent criminal records and sex offender registries.

7. Consider a mother or father who cares for the happiness of his or her child. Parents have been known to make enormous sacrifices for their children, from sleep to their social lives, and to endure financial costs to make their children happy.

8. Giacomo Rizzolatti and Laila Craighero, "The Mirror-Neuron System," *Annual Review of Neuroscience* 27 (2004): 169–92.

9. "The capacity for making moral decisions is innate—the sympathetic circuit is hard-wired, at least in most of us—but it still requires the right kind of experience in order to develop," from Jonah Lehrer, *How We Decide* (Boston: Houghton Mifflin Harcourt, 2009), 188.

10. Jean-Paul Sartre, *Existentialism and Humanism* (Paris: Methuen, 1948).

CHAPTER 10: SOCIETAL HAPPINESS

1. Okay, not exactly. Technically voters in the United States vote for electors in the Electoral College, who in turn vote for the candidates. But in practice, the result has been the same. So far.

2. Colossians 3:22 (New Living Translation).

3. For example, the Athenian democracy around 550 BCE used a lottery system to decide which citizens would serve in which government positions.

4. It should be noted that we differ from Harris in some ways when it comes to his views about "moral truth" or "moral realism." Harris asserts that we can ascertain facts about morality through biology, chemistry, or neuroscience. He argues that just as we can research the chemistry of the food to determine if it is more or less healthy for us, so too can physiological knowledge yield objective facts about morality. In the food example, we would contend that facts about the nutritional value of food are legitimate forms of knowledge, but they only produce objective facts about what to eat if we assume that nutrition is the overriding purpose of consuming food. That isn't always the case. Much of the time we consume food for taste (such as at a fine restaurant), paying little attention to the nutritional content of the food. For many of us, nutrition is often a secondary concern, so the facts do not create an objective preference. Prioritizing between taste and nutrition turns out to be a preference, just as balancing one's personal desires and one's "well-being" is ultimately a preference. So while we might be able to easily demonstrate that stealing is highly correlated with imprisonment as a fact, when a thief contemplates whether or not to steal, the thief's appetite for risk is a preference-based decision. Even if objective facts might be useful in predicting expected outcomes of an attempted heist, there still exists no "moral truth" to determine what the risk appetite of the thief "should" be.

5. Sociopathy is another area of moral concern that raises interesting questions. Just because some psychologically deviant people commit ethical atrocities like murder or rape doesn't mean that we can't expect reasonable adults to adhere to certain basic moral principles. It merely highlights the fact that not everyone is psychologically healthy (some people lack innate empathy) or has the ability to make

rational decisions regarding the life-happiness of others or even of themselves. We react in shock and disbelief when atrocities are committed by seemingly "normal" people because we find it so unfathomable that someone who appeared reasonable—someone who it seemed should be in touch with these ethical principles— could ever take such actions.

6. PolitiFact, "Obama's More Right Than He Knows," http://www.politifact .com/truth-o-meter/statements/2008/apr/15/barack-obama/obamas-more-right -than-he-knows.

7. Indeed, some of our laws have nothing to do with morality, such as laws that establish that we drive on the right-hand side of the road. After all, motorists in the United Kingdom and Japan drive on the left-hand side with equal success. On the other hand, many past laws around ethics are immoral by the ethical standards of today. Examples in the United States include laws banning interracial or same-sex marriage. At the same time, many immoral acts aren't illegal by law. Consider that the UK government only recently (in the last thirty years) made spousal rape a punishable crime.

CHAPTER 11: PUTTING ETHICAL BELIEFS TO THE TEST

1. Judith Jarvis Thomson, "The Trolley Problem," *Yale Law Journal* 94, no. 6 (1985): 1395–415.

2. Another classic example of an impossible clash of absolute principles: "What happens when an unstoppable force meets an immovable object?" The solution involves dismantling the absolutes. If there is such a thing as an unstoppable force, there can't exist such a thing as an immovable object, and vice versa.

3. K.I.N.D., http://www.msnbc.com/kind-fund.

4. This topic was explored in Charles Darwin's *On the Origin of Species*, chapter 8, "Instinct. Objections to the Theory of Natural Selection as Applied to Instincts: Neuter and Sterile Insects" (London: John Murray, 1859). See also R. A. Fisher, *The Genetical Theory of Natural Selection* (Oxford: Clarendon Press, 1930): 159; and W. D. Hamilton, "The Genetical Evolution of Social Behavior," *Journal of Theoretical Biology* 7, no. 1 (1964): 1–16.

5. There are a few parallels here with a branch of moral philosophy called "care ethics," which views morality through the lens of human relationships and the context of social interactions. However, care ethics differs from the subjective moral theory we are describing in that it sees caregiving as the fundamental driver of morals, whereas we see a person's happiness preferences as the main moral driver.

6. Innocence Project, "DNA Exoneration Nationwide," http://www.innocen ceproject.org/Content/DNA_Exonerations_Nationwide.php.

7. John Eligon and Michael Copper. "Blasts at Boston Marathon Kill 3 and Injure 100," *New York Times*, April 15, 2013.

8. Grand jury indictment, http://cache.boston.com/multimedia/2013/06/27indictment/tsarnaev.pdf.

9. The Chesterton quote provides a final, ironic proof of this concept because, as it turns out, Chesterton never said it. The source was Belgian playwright Émile Cammaerts, writing in a book about Chesterton. But because people preferred that the quote come from the famous theologian rather than a little-known playwright, it was quickly misattributed, and the error was passed down through the years uncorrected, like countless other unexamined beliefs.

CHAPTER 12: FINDING YOUR OWN NON-COMMANDMENTS

1. William Shakespeare, *Hamlet* (1602), act 2, scene 2.

APPENDIX A: COMMON RELIGIOUS OBJECTIONS

1. Parts of this chapter, as well as parts of the introduction, come from a paper titled "On religion" written by the author, Lex Bayer, in a writing class at Stanford University.

2. John Hick, *God and the Universe of Faiths* (London: Macmillan, 1973), 140.

3. David Hume, Section X, "Of Miracles," in *An Enquiry Concerning Human Understanding* (New York: Oxford University Press, 1999).

4. Blaise Pascal, *Pensées*, trans. A. J. Krailsheimer (New York: Penguin Books, 1995). See also Jeff Jordan, *Pascal's Wager: Pragmatic Arguments and Belief in God* (Oxford, UK: Oxford University Press, 2006).

5. James Cargile, "Pascal's Wager," in *Contemporary Philosophy of Religion*, ed. Steven M. Cahn and David Shatz (New York: Oxford University Press, 1982).

6. Exodus 3:2.

7. Joshua 10:13.

8. Matthew 14:22–33.

9. From David Hume, *An Enquiry Concerning Human Understanding* (New York: Oxford University Press, 1999), 74.

10. Joshua 10:13.

11. John 10:11.

12. Sam Harris, *The Moral Landscape: How Science Can Determine Human Values* (New York: Free Press, 2010), 138.

13. Harris, *Moral Landscape*, 139.

14. Legatum Institute, "Legatum Prosperity Index," http://www.prosperity.com/#!.

15. Gallup Global Reports, "What Alabamians and Iranians Have in Common," http://www.gallup.com/poll/114211/Alabamians-Iranians-Common.aspx.

16. For an example of such a situation, see Liz Szabo, "Doctor Accused of Selling False Hope to Families," *USA Today*, January 8, 2014.

17. Ewan Palmer, "Russia Road Accident Baby Dies after Parents Choose 'Emergency Baptism' over Hospital," *International Business Times*, November 28, 2013.

18. Francis Bacon, *Meditationes Sacrae* (1597).

BIBLIOGRAPHY

Aristotle. *Aristotle's Nicomachean Ethics.* Translated by Joe Sachs. Newbury, MA: Focus/R. Pullins, 2002.

Armstrong, Karen. *A History of God: The 4,000-Year Quest of Judaism, Christianity, and Islam.* New York: A.A. Knopf, 1993.

Bentham, Jeremy. *The Principles of Morals and Legislation.* Buffalo, NY: Prometheus Books, 1988.

Bok, Hilary. *Freedom and Responsibility.* Princeton, NJ: Princeton University Press, 1998.

Bueno de Mesquita, Bruce. *The Predictioneer's Game: Using the Logic of Brazen Self-Interest to See and Shape the Future.* New York: Random House, 2009.

Camus, Albert. *The Plague.* New York: Modern Library, 1948.

Dawkins, Richard. *Climbing Mount Improbable.* New York: Norton, 1996.

———. *River Out of Eden: A Darwinian View of Life.* New York: Basic Books, 1995.

———. *The Ancestor's Tale: A Pilgrimage to the Dawn of Evolution.* Boston: Houghton Mifflin, 2004.

———. *The Blind Watchmaker: Why the Evidence of Evolution Reveals a Universe without Design.* New York: Norton, 1986.

———. *The God Delusion.* Boston: Houghton Mifflin, 2006.

———. *The Greatest Show on Earth: The Evidence for Evolution.* New York: Free Press, 2009.

———. *The Selfish Gene.* Oxford, UK: Oxford University Press, 1989.

Dennett, Daniel Clement. *Elbow Room: The Varieties of Free Will Worth Wanting.* Cambridge, MA: MIT Press, 1984.

———. *Freedom Evolves.* New York: Viking, 2003.

———. *The Intentional Stance.* Cambridge, MA: MIT Press, 1987.

———. *Kinds of Minds: Toward an Understanding of Consciousness.* New York: Basic Books, 1996.

Epstein, Greg M. *Good without God: What a Billion Nonreligious People Do Believe.* New York: William Morrow, 2009.

Gilligan, Carol. *In a Different Voice: Psychological Theory and Women's Development.* Cambridge, MA: Harvard University Press, 1982.

Haidt, Jonathan. *The Righteous Mind: Why Good People Are Divided by Politics and Religion.* New York: Vintage, 2013.

Harris, Sam. *Free Will.* New York: Free Press, 2012.

———. *The End of Faith: Religion, Terror, and the Future of Reason.* New York: W. W. Norton, 2004.

———. *Letter to a Christian Nation.* New York: Knopf, 2006.

———. *The Moral Landscape: How Science Can Determine Human Values.* New York: Free Press, 2010.

Hitchens, Christopher. *God Is Not Great: How Religion Poisons Everything.* New York: Twelve, 2007.

———. *Hitch-22: A Memoir.* New York: Twelve, 2010.

———. *The Missionary Position: Mother Teresa in Theory and Practice.* London: Verso, 1995.

———. *Mortality.* New York: Twelve, 2012.

———. *The Portable Atheist: Essential Readings for the Nonbeliever.* Philadelphia: Da Capo, 2007.

Hobbes, Thomas. *Leviathan.* Edited and with an introduction by J. C. A. Gaskin. Oxford, UK: Oxford University Press, 1998.

Hume, David. *Dialogues Concerning Natural Religion in Focus.* Edited by Stanley Tweyman. London: Routledge, 1991.

———. *A Treatise of Human Nature.* 2nd ed. Edited by L. A. Selby-Bigge. Revised by P. H. Nidditch. Oxford, UK: Clarendon Press, 1978.

———. *An Enquiry Concerning Human Understanding.* Edited by Tom L. Beauchamp. New York: Oxford University Press, 1999.

Jewish Publication Society of America. *The Torah: The Five Books of Moses.* 1st ed. Philadelphia: Jewish Publication Society of America, 1963.

John Templeton Foundation. *Does Science Make Belief in God Obsolete? Thirteen Views on the Question.* West Conshohocken, PA: John Templeton Foundation, 2008.

Jordan, Michael. *Dictionary of Gods and Goddesses.* 2nd ed. New York: Facts on File, 2004.

Kant, Immanuel. *Groundwork for the Metaphysics of Morals.* Edited and translated by Allen W. Wood. New Haven, CT: Yale University Press, 2002.

Kant, Immanuel. *Critique of Practical Reason.* Translated by Werner S. Pluhar. Introduction by Stephen Engstrom. Indianapolis: Hackett, 2002.

———. *Critique of Pure Reason.* Edited, translated, and with an introduction by Marcus Weigelt. London: Penguin, 2007.

———. *Prolegomena to Any Future Metaphysics and the Letter to Marcus Herz, February 1772.* 2nd ed. Edited and translated by James W. Ellington. Indianapolis: Hackett, 2010.

Kushner, Harold S. *When Bad Things Happen to Good People: With a New Preface by the Author.* 20th anniversary ed. New York: Schocken Books, 2001.

Kymlicka, Will. *Contemporary Political Philosophy: An Introduction.* Oxford, UK: Clarendon Press, 1990.

Lehrer, Jonah. *How We Decide.* Boston: Houghton Mifflin Harcourt, 2009.

Leibniz, Gottfried Wilhelm. *Theodicy: Essays on the Goodness of God, the Freedom of Man, and the Origin of Evil.* Edited and with an introduction by Austin Farrer. Translated by E. M. Huggard. London: Routledge & Kegan Paul, 1951.

Locke, John. *Two Treatises of Government.* Student ed. Edited by Peter Laslett. Cambridge, UK: Cambridge University Press, 1988.

———. *An Essay Concerning Human Understanding.* Edited by Alexander Campbell Fraser. New York: Dover Publications, 1959.

Mill, John Stuart. *The Basic Writings of John Stuart Mill: On Liberty, the Subjection of Women, and Utilitarianism.* New York: Modern Library, 2002.

Norman, Richard. *On Humanism.* London: Routledge, 2004.

Perry, John. *A Dialogue on Personal Identity and Immorality.* Indianapolis: Hackett, 1978.

Pinker, Steven. *The Better Angels of Our Nature: Why Violence Has Declined.* New York: Viking, 2011.

Plato. *Plato: Euthyphro, Apology, Crito, Phaedo, Phaedrus.* Translated by Harold North Fowler. Cambridge, MA: Harvard University Press, 1990.

Russell, Bertrand. *The Problems of Philosophy.* 2nd ed. Introduction by John Skorupski. Oxford: Oxford University Press, 1998.

Sartre, Jean-Paul. *Existentialism Is a Humanism.* Edited by John Kulka. Introduction by Arlette Elkaïm-Sartre. New Haven, CT: Yale University Press, 2007.

Simon, Herbert A. *Models of Bounded Rationality.* Cambridge, MA: MIT Press, 1982.

———. *Models of Man: Social and Rational.* New York: Wiley, 1957.

———. *Reason in Human Affairs.* Stanford, CA: Stanford University Press, 1983.

Singer, Peter. *How Are We to Live? Ethics in an Age of Self-Interest.* Amherst, NY: Prometheus Books, 1995.

———. *Practical Ethics.* Cambridge, UK: Cambridge University Press, 1979.

Spong, John Shelby. *Why Christianity Must Change or Die: A Bishop Speaks to Believers in Exile.* San Francisco, CA: HarperSanFrancisco, 1998.

Thomson, J. Anderson, Clare Aukofer, and Richard Dawkins. *Why We Believe in God(s): A Concise Guide to the Science of Faith.* Charlottesville, VA: Pitchstone, 2011.

Watson, Gary, ed. *Free Will.* 2nd ed. New York: Oxford University Press, 2003.

INDEX

absolutes, 32, 83, 112, 166n2
afterlife, 61. *See also* heaven, hell,
   reincarnation
agnostics, 9–12
assumptions, 20–23, 28–29, 124, 140,
   142; of a God, 53–55, 132–35; of
   external reality, 23–24, 140,142;
   of using our minds, 26–28, 140,
   142; of using our senses, 24–26,
   140, 142; tools for evaluating,
   21–23
atheists, 2–5, 9–12, 158n3. *See also*
   nonbelievers
authority, 13, 77, 87, 146

Bayer, Lex, 1, 6, 59–61, 115–18
behavior, 65–69, 71–74, 77–78, 92;
   duty and, 88–89; effect of religion
   on, 47, 98; motivation for, 65–66,
   68, 71–72; rules of behavior (laws),
   108
belief, paradox of, 19–20; turtle
   parable, 19–20, 55
beliefs: change of, 34, 36–38, 145;
   confidence in, 32–34; factual, 23,
   57; framework of, 28; inductive,
   31–32, 35; in God, 2–5, 10–11,
   47–48, 52–56, 134–38; justification

of, 12, 19–20, 27, 36, 38; societal
   benefits of, 137–38; theorem of, 29,
   141–52; unjustifiable, 20–21
believers, religious, 11–12, 74, 129,
   134–35
believing (act of), 32–33, 43–44,
   129–36, 144–45
Bentham, Jeremy, 87, 146
Bible, 4, 12–14, 51, 131, 134–35,
   158n10
brain, 61, 71–72, 82–83, 96

charity, 6, 84, 96, 108, 114
Chesterton, Gilbert Keith (G. K.), 2,
   121
choices, 78–79; conflicting, 37–38, 69;
   consequences of, 87, 113; effect
   of, 79; illusion of choice, 79–80;
   motivation for, 81, 93, 99, 113
Christianity, 3, 49–50, 135
Church of Jesus Christ of Latter-Day
   Saints. *See* Mormonism
comforts (psychological), 2, 11, 113,
   123, 135–36
commandments (religious), 9, 12–15,
   83–84, 120
commitments, 88–89, 97
community, 13, 15, 85, 94

ABOUT THE AUTHORS

Lex Bayer grew up in the suburbs of Johannesburg, South Africa, where he attended a secular Jewish day school from kindergarten through high school. He moved to the United States for college. At Stanford University he received his undergraduate and master's degrees in engineering while also being a member of the Stanford men's soccer team and Stanford debate team.

In his professional life, Lex is an inventor and technology entrepreneur. He holds more than twenty patents in diverse fields ranging from inertial sensors and software algorithms to consumer products and medical devices. He was the CEO and cofounder of a payments software company that grew to service five million customers and was ultimately acquired by Visa Inc. Lex has been a panelist and speaker at a number of social networking and web 2.0 conferences.

Lex serves as a board member of the Humanist Connection, a humanist, atheist, and agnostic nonprofit organization serving Stanford University and Silicon Valley. He lives in Menlo Park, California.

John P. Figdor is the humanist chaplain serving the atheist, humanist, and agnostic communities at Stanford University. He organizes events and programs for both students and community members from the San Francisco Bay Area, provides officiant services and humanist counseling, and advocates for the secular perspective both on campus and off. John and his work have been discussed in the *New York Times*, the *Washington Post*, and the *San Francisco Chronicle*. He is a regular guest on *Huffington Post Live* on issues around nonbelief. He is a frequent speaker at secular conferences and local humanist groups across the United States. He received his bachelor's degree with honors in philosophy from Vassar College and holds a master's degree (MDiv) in humanism and interfaith dialogue from Harvard Divinity School—the first of its kind and the pilot program for the humanist chaplain training program at Harvard. John was an organizing fellow of the humanist chaplaincy at Harvard, and after he graduated he was later appointed to be the assistant humanist chaplain at Harvard, where he served until becoming the humanist chaplain at Stanford in 2012.

A transplanted New Yorker, he lives and works in the San Francisco Bay Area in California.